VINTAGE
LIVING

VINTAGE LIVING

Creating a Beautiful Home with Treasured Objects from the Past

BOB RICHTER

RIZZOLI
NEW YORK

New York · Paris · London · Milan

TABLE OF CONTENTS

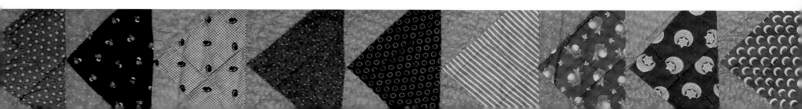

Dedication

For my family, especially Mom and Robin, who taught me the meaning of emotional value.

For those who believe in me and support me on this journey of *Vintage Living*: Sharon, Amy, Mollie, Blake, Dan, Clint, Christina, Chuck, Matt, Jay, Christopher, Eldin, Karl, Kim, Mary Margaret, and Sefton.

For those who've crossed over: Nana, Johnny, Walter, Sunny, and Dad—you are alive in my work every day. Thanks to all of you for the roots and wings.

And for the beautiful people of the Delaware River towns and everyone who loves and lives with treasured objects from the past—thank you!

INTRODUCTION

✳ Bob Richter ✳

My journey into *Vintage Living* began in the attic of my family's home. Ours was a treasure trove and a history lesson. By age six, the antiques buff, decorator and historian in me were alive and well, making discoveries and taking notes.

I began unearthing forgotten family antiques, bringing them back into the light of day and arranging them in my bedroom. My nana saw the decorating spark in me and decided to light the fire. As the matriarch of our family's interior design business, she brought me with her to visit clients, many of whom lived with beautiful antiques. I'd haul fabric samples; hold the ladder when nana measured, etc. What I received in return was a vision of what was possible. And what a great gift that was.

Nana had an incredible grasp of color and always switched out slipcovers and drapes with the seasons. She also had many wonderful things from my Great Uncle Gerber's import store. Gerber's wife Eve once gave me a trio of bronze "See No Evil, Hear No Evil, Say No Evil" monkeys that soon sparked a collection--something that happens when vintage objects are gifted with love.

With money I'd earned at the family business, I was able to begin hunting for more vintage finds. My big brother, Johnny, became my inspiration and guide and would take me to flea markets, yard sales and thrift stores. He taught me that buying vintage was fun, interesting and personal.

Soon my mom let me incorporate my finds into the rest of our house. One was a beautiful mantle clock I had discovered in the attic and that my siblings and I got repaired and gave her for Christmas. Mom wound it weekly and doing so became a chance for us to slow down and connect. Soon a portrait of her grandfather (also stored in the attic for decades) was added to the mix. I learned that he was a gentle, loving man who had a great impact on her. The stories she began telling me about him brought us even closer together.

These family objects were the seedlings for the core principles of *Vintage Living*—comfort, connection and continuity. They added a palpable comfort to our home. Discussing them and sharing them, we felt connection. Living with them, they added continuity to our lives.

Drawing on my sister Robin's and my nana's expertise, I learned how to renovate old things with new fabrics and finishes. Our home went from looking dated (1970s) to timeless (a mix of old and new). It taught me that if you surround yourself with what you love, your home never goes out of style.

When I left for college I brought vintage pieces that reminded me of home. My dorm room at New York University was appointed with vintage lamps, rugs, art and other décor, along with drapes and bedding made by nana. The look on people's faces after they'd walked down the fluorescently lit cinderblock hallways into "Bobby's Boudoir" was priceless.

Soon I began working for a magnificent New York antiques dealer named Sunny. Over the years, she generously passed along her vast knowledge to me and it added another priceless layer to my life and work.

I've had many dwellings since that dorm room, but all share one thing in common—objects that create a feeling of being home. That's what *Vintage Living* is all about. Most of my friends know this well. You'll some of their beautiful homes on the following pages. I hope this book inspires you to honor those treasures that add comfort, connection and continuity to your home.

Enjoy Vintage Living!

PAGE 3: *The square floral pillows on this chaise longue in my living room were made by my grandmother and were on her sofa for decades. My sister made the round and rectangular pillows from vintage fabric from my grandmother's workroom.*
OPPOSITE: *My great uncle and aunt, Gerber and Eve, owned an import store filled with global treasures like this temple god I found years ago at a flea market. The vendor told me it came from Allentown, Pennsylvania (my hometown), so I thought there was a chance he could be from their store. Now he sits in the corner of my bedroom. Around his neck is my great grandfather's watch fob, which my grandmother turned into a necklace (they had the same initials), and my grandmother's charm necklace. The silver baby shoe charm has my name and birthday engraved on it.*

chapter one

CREATING A SENSE OF PLACE

Bob Richter's 1859 Italianate Home

reating a sense of place has always been deeply important to me. Decorating with vintage pieces adds texture and history—and it also personalizes a home. This historic Italianate town house won my heart the minute I walked in the door and it has easily become my most beloved personal project to date. While built in 1859, its lines are modern, its moldings are sublime, and its natural light is bountiful. With glorious pocket doors, a spacious window seat, leaded glass windows, and four porches to create outdoor rooms, finding it sent me straight to seventh heaven. As I walked though, I saw my favorite finds here, I saw endless possibilities, and I knew where all the Christmas trees would go.

The previous owners took painstaking efforts to preserve all of its historic charm, while making mindful updates. For them, this sale was deeply personal because the home had been in their family for eighty-three years. I'm proud to say that we are good friends today and I'm profoundly grateful to them for all that they've done to help me and to educate me about the home. They even went so far as to list it on the National Register of Historic Places and present me with that wonderful plaque to ensure that this special place is always honored and protected. I truly feel I'm more caretaker than homeowner. Any changes I make, I want them to look as if they've always been here.

I believe in honoring the past, but not living in it. So I had no interest in decorating a home from the mid-1800s with furnishings from that time period. For me it's all about the lines and the colors. The triangular moldings and room layouts are perfect backdrops to my vintage pieces, many of which were inherited from my family. While I mix all decades, my favorite furnishings are from the 1920s through the 1950s. Even though it is a new place for me, it has great history and I am now a part of it. Putting down roots here means bringing much-loved vintage pieces and family heirlooms into every room.

And of course a home is also about location, location, location. Mine happens to be in the middle of one of my favorite places on earth, with wonderful shops, restaurants, and neighbors—all navigable by foot. It's a progressive Mayberry—where all are welcome. In this day and age, it's where I want to hang my hat.

PAGE 8: *This mid-century modern chair has been with me for a long time and has lived in several of my homes. For its new chapter, I tapped my talented upholsterer Eldin to cover it in men's suiting fabric I found at a thrift store. I found the circular ottoman at a flea market and added it to the mix. Another flea market find, the painting by Harriet Boyd, was done in 1950 and is an all-time favorite. The subjects are like sentinels and their expressions are sublime.* ABOVE: *I've found this passage in many incarnations in many flea markets. It's a verse from the Bible (John 14:1) and this version is reverse painted on glass. No matter your religious background, it's a comforting message and one that clearly people needed to hear—and still do. I keep it in my bedroom.*

LEFT: *This vintage Turkish lamp belonged to my grandparents—a fortieth wedding anniversary present from my great uncle and aunt, who owned the import store. As a child I loved it and when the time was right, my grandmother decided it should be mine. It holds great emotional value for me, so I placed it in front of a mirror in my living room where its beauty is doubled.*
BELOW: *Detail on the well-worn antique Iranian rug in the sitting room—easily the oldest furnishing in the room—always feels fresh, no matter how many times it's been repaired.*

PREVIOUS SPREAD: *The mid-century sofa was orange when I found it at a flea market; I reupholstered it in moss green mohair. I had bolsters made to both soften the lines and add comfort. The colorful Turkish lamp belonged to my grandmother; I always loved it and she gave it to me when I had my first real apartment. The modernist painting of dancers came from a little antiques shop in New York's West Village. I admired it for months, when one day it was gone. Italian* Vogue *had rented it for a shoot. Happily for me, they paid well so the dealer sold it to me at a bargain price.* OPPOSITE: *I have reading nooks all over the house and this one doubles as a spot to have a leisurely phone call. It's also the closest thing I have to a gift-wrap room. The roll of paper under the table was found in a general store. The paper on top is my go-to all-occasion vintage wrap.* ABOVE: *I found this small art deco writing desk in an antiques shop in upstate New York. I love how its angular lines play with the moldings in my home. The spherical wooden lamp is from Portes de Vanves flea market in Paris and the 1930s Wolfgang Hoffmann streamlined tubular cocktail table is from the Chelsea Flea in New York.*

ABOVE: *I love both Santa Fe, New Mexico, and Moab, Utah, and this painting, which hangs above the mantel in my sitting room, reminds me of both. On either side are art deco statues I purchased from my friend Judy. I love them individually but even more so as a pair. The bronze deer on marble bases, like everything else in the photo, came from a flea market.* OPPOSITE: *The French art deco chandelier is from Clignancourt flea market in Paris, and now resides in my sitting room. The bronze-ball lamps are from an antiques shop in upstate New York. I married them with simple, contemporary shades, which allows their great lines and color to pop. Vintage paintings from local artists hang above.*

I like to say this large harlequin painting actually found me. The artist was clearly influenced by Picasso and I was immediately drawn to it. When I looked in the corner and saw the signature, I was blown away: Waldo Angelo was the best friend of my antiques mentor, Sunny. I already owned other pieces of his work, so of course this had to come home with me.

chapter one **CREATING A SENSE OF PLACE**

I'm told that hanging artwork salon style can be intimidating, although I don't find it so. It's simply a logical by-product of having a lot of stuff. It has to go somewhere! I particularly like to hang art this way in staircases and this view showcases a few of my favorite pieces. The chestnut balusters are original to the house and the art plays with them nicely.

PREVIOUS SPREAD: *When you have a lot of stuff, symmetry and color can harmonize it. This view of my bed showcases the concept. I particularly love the punch of the 1970s ginger jar lamps: the pair was a whopping ninety cents at a thrift store. As much as I love all things vintage, I always buy a new bed. This basic headboard has great lines and allows the other objects to be the stars of the show.* ABOVE: *When I found this painting it was rolled up and had been tucked away for years. In fact, if you look closely, you'll see it's unfinished. I think he has a quiet strength, so I decided to find him a proper vintage frame. The vase belonged to my nana; she used to keep her umbrella in it near the front door. The gold "B" is a nod to my inner Mary Tyler Moore.* OPPOSITE: *The art deco furniture in my bedroom is from a thrift store near my mom's house. I went bananas for the confluence of wooden and chrome inlays. The hand-carved wooden foxes are from the Black Forest region of Germany. The man in the kimono is Bob: after he passed, the women organizing his estate sale asked me if I would adopt him and I gladly obliged.*

chapter one **CREATING A SENSE OF PLACE**

OPPPOSITE: *I use a lot of mirrors because they reflect light and give interesting perspectives into art and other objects. This gilt mirror reflects a painting I brought home from Barcelona. The Moorish nightlight belonged to my nana and is surrounded by a number of my favorite pieces of art pottery.*
ABOVE: *Many people say brown wood is passé, but I wholeheartedly disagree. I have such pieces from all periods, from Empire to art deco. I think they add a great deal of warmth and permanence to my home. They also do a great job of containing sweaters, off-season clothing, and paperwork. The angel Christmas ornament was made by my best friend Sharon and hangs on the knob of this cabinet all year long.*

PREVIOUS SPREAD: *The guest room showcases my grandparents' bedroom furniture and my sister Robin's prowess as a master seamstress. As a young boy I loved the lines and colors of this 1930s suite. When I moved it to my home, I looked for fabric that would complement it nicely. This vintage chintz came from an interior designer friend who decorated the White House twice over. Robin got the hard job . . . creating all of the custom window treatments and bedding.* ABOVE AND OPPOSITE: *While the guest room is small in size, it has four doors and lots of light so it feels very welcoming. In fact, when I don't have company, I spend a great deal of time here. It's a room that truly provides comfort, connection, and continuity with its vintage decor.*

For me, a kitchen must be joyful and "kitchenalia" is one of my favorite categories of collecting. Fresh-cut lilacs from my backyard sit atop a 1930s bench covered with fun geometric linoleum. A mid-century pixie sits in his shelf above my coffee maker. Around the fridge are a few of my favorite finds from international flea markets (Budapest, Berlin, Amsterdam, and Paris). The grilled cheese sign is from an old Woolworth's five-and-ten, a store that conjures up a lot of happy childhood memories.

FOLLOWING SPREAD: *The large marble island in the kitchen is perfect for displaying favorite vintage kitchen pieces. My sister Robin used every square inch of the fanciful 1930s floral fabric I found to create panels and valances for the windows. A favorite family piece hangs in the upper left-hand corner: an art deco pie dish that my mom passed along to me. Every time I see it I think of corn pies, cherry tarts, and other delights from her kitchen. The vintage perpetual calendar is one of many around my home. I find that they help me be a bit more mindful at the start of each day.*

You are only as big as the DREAM you dare to live

My favorite vintage kitchen pieces are typically from the 1920s to '40s. The coffee canister belonged to my nana—given to her by my mom when she was a little girl—so it holds great sentimental value. The Dutch tea canister is a nod to nana's roots. The celluloid aviator was meant to hold a pen, but he displays a matchbook from a favorite New York restaurant that closed several years ago. The little green pickle on wheels has been with me since I was a little boy.

This metal "What we Need" sign once hung inside a Boone kitchen cabinet. I love how the little plastic knobs were designed to slide to designate which items should be added to the shopping list: it's also a great window into how simple needs were at one time. (And don't forget to pick up some lard!)

I believe in the importance of a dining room, so naturally when I walked in and saw the original built-in china cabinet it was love at first sight. The furniture belonged to my grandparents and I treasure it. I found the lemon-lime striped draperies at Clignancourt flea market in Paris and had them in my New York living room for years. For this home, I shortened them and had just enough fabric left to cover the chairs. My mom gets a kick out of the vintage bocce balls in the center bowl. I call them my visual potpourri. FOLLOWING SPREAD: Since the dining room is rather small, I hung the large mirror over the buffet to open up the space. The buffet is a place for me to have fun color blocking favorite pieces of art pottery. I found the chandelier globes at an auction and married them to a new fixture with the right lines and proportions for the room. The wall sconces are from the Moravian Tile Works in Doylestown, Pennsylvania.

ABOVE: *The architectural details of this house are sparingly ornate, one of the things I love about the Italianate style. The hand-carved scrollwork on the side porches gives just enough of that something extra for the eye to enjoy. The center columns also feature some charming, intricate detail.* OPPOSITE: *This second-floor porch was originally an outdoor room and it's one of my favorite places in the whole house. I actually wrote the majority of this book in this very spot. All the vintage wicker furniture was found at flea markets. I covered the cushions with new awning stripe material that complements the wonderful painted details.*

The architectural details around town are relatively simple, yet charming. Most buildings hail from the mid-1800s before Victorian architecture went wild. I love the restrained yet elegant feel of the homes. Small businesses thrive here and all are welcome at every house of worship. It really is a modern-day Mayberry.

chapter two

A JOURNEY OF OBJECTS

*What Comes with Me from
My City Apartment to My New
Small Town Home?*

When I purchased my "new" home, I envisioned many of my favorite things would make the trip from big city to country city, small apartment to big house, but deciding what pieces would make the cut was truly a sentimental journey. Family pieces are a given, as is my beloved art collection. For me these objects are all about creating comfort, connection, and continuity in a home.

I also envisioned many of those furnishings defining areas of the new space and taking on new life. The mid-century chair from my New York City bedroom is now in the sitting room and I had it covered in blue pinstriped suiting material. The art deco glass block mantel from my previous living room is now in my TV room. More rooms mean more chances to play, and that's my idea of a good time.

My New York City kitchen was designed around the Riviera china I inherited from the antiques dealer who mentored me for so many years. I used the wonderful colors to pull in stained glass windows, green countertops, vintage knobs, and an orange refrigerator. I also chose glass front cabinet doors to showcase my collection. For the country city home, the previous owners did a wonderful job with the kitchen renovation, so it was move-in ready. Since the backdrop is so plain, all of my multicolored kitchenalia really pops. My sister used 1920s vintage fabric I found to make panels for the windows, which define the space.

The late-1800s armoire from my city bedroom is now here in my dressing room. The decorative triangular lines mirror those of the moldings in the house and the fact that this place is big enough for a dressing room makes me do a happy dance.

One of the most rewarding things for me about the new space was the opportunity to bring in so many of my grandmother's pieces of furniture I'd had in storage for years, including her dining room furniture and bedroom suite (now being enjoyed by visitors to my guest room—and me when I want to switch things up!).

PAGE 44: *The bench in my dressing room originally belonged to my great grandmother, then it resided in my Aunt Vivian's foyer for another forty years. She passed it along to me when I moved into my new home. It's the perfect spot for me to put on my shoes in the morning.* ABOVE: *My grandmother made this needlepoint tiger as a gift for my grandfather. It originally hung in a frame, but when it was passed along to me, my sister turned it into a pillow—which I love. The bedroom rug originally belonged to my friend Stephen, who designed it for his apartment. When he moved he changed color palettes and asked me if I'd like to have it. Naturally the answer was yes!* OPPOSITE: *I move things around regularly—it's my idea of a good time. This corner has seen a lot of incarnations and this one showcases a modernist dandelion sculpture in the manner of Harry Bertoia. The fanciful deer watercolor, from the People's Store in Lambertville, New Jersey, is the one constant.*

PREVIOUS SPREAD: *My art deco glass block and chrome mantel as it now resides in the TV room. Above it hangs a painting of one of my favorite actresses, Gene Tierney, done by my friend Sioux Krause. The chair to the left was originally in the waiting area of our family business in the 1950s and the chair to the right belonged to my antiques mentor, Sunny.* THIS SPREAD: *Here's the art deco mantel as it was in my New York City apartment. The electric candelabra came from Clingnancourt flea market in Paris. The bulbous teal vases are from the 1930s Futura line by Roseville. Those vases have since made their way to the living room mantel in my new home—in front of which is a radiator, so I had my carpenter build a surround to match the existing moldings. If I'm to add anything new to a home's architecture (interior or exterior), I want it to look as if it's always been there.*

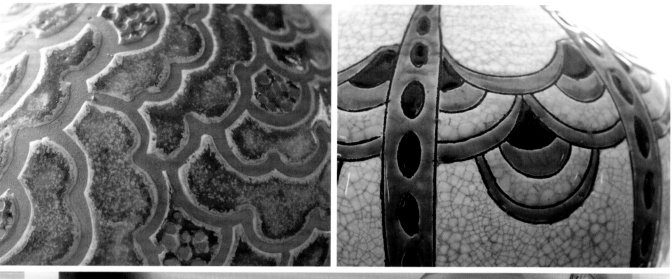

This is another corner that changes with my moods and the seasons. The burled wood Italian art deco table is from Midiri Antiques in Lambertville, New Jersey. The English urn-style lamp is from Housing Works Thrift Shop in New York. The small vases have a silver inlay and can be seen as they once resided on a shelf in my old apartment. I'm continually inspired by the wonderful lines and colors of my pottery collection, most of which is French and Belgian, and they often guide my palette for a room.

ABOVE: *I am in love with this mid-century Brutalist lamp, acquired from the estate of a woman with incredible, eclectic taste. In front is a French art deco chair (one of a pair) from the People's Store in Lambertville, New Jersey. The RCA stereo is a constant and follows me whereever I go.* OPPOSITE: *A glimpse into the corner of my New York City bedroom, which had dark brown walls. Many of these pieces have since made their way to my new home, which has a brighter backdrop and more rooms, so they've been split up.*

I acquired the "Powder Room" sign many years ago from a funeral home that was going out of business. It has traveled with me through three different homes and is always one of the first things I hang when I set up housekeeping. The blue mirrored glass, chrome mounts, and sensational lettering all scream art deco. I love the Old Hollywood feel it embodies.

The Parisian taxi sign was a New York City flea market find and brings to mind many fond memories. In my old apartment I kept it propped up behind the stove to add a pop of whimsy. The hand-painted bit of wisdom is always a good reminder. The art deco ceiling fixture is from a Czech antiques dealer and friend; it was perfect for this kitchen, but now it resides in the TV room of my new home. Think you can't make an impact in a small kitchen? Think again! I pulled colors from my favorite set of china and just had fun. The custom stained-glass window offers both beauty and privacy.

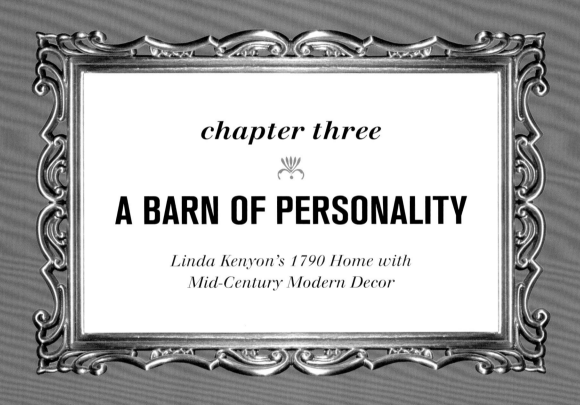

chapter three

A BARN OF PERSONALITY

*Linda Kenyon's 1790 Home with
Mid-Century Modern Decor*

Depending on the day you visit Linda Kenyon in her wonderful 1790s home, you might also meet Eleanor Roosevelt or Julia Child. The actress routinely channels them for theater performances and comes home after a show still in character. The day we photographed, it was Julia who arrived as we were working. The "Bon Appetit" trivet hanging among her copper pots in the kitchen is a nod to that recurring role. When the wig and makeup come off, however, Linda has a charming, welcoming personality all her own and her home is a reflection of that.

Linda's father, a set designer, found the property in 1963 and at the time it was a barn and a farmhouse. "It was a derelict, a wreck . . . and a project worth taking on," were the words Linda recalled her father saying when he talked about the home. His idea was to bring the outside in, so there is a lot of stone and natural wood. Also, whenever possible, all original pieces like the barn doors and hardware were salvaged and restored. Clearly Linda's father knew what he was talking about because by 1965 it was featured on the cover of the September issue of *House Beautiful*.

With wonderful exposed beams and stucco walls, the home feels like an English country manor. Inside, Linda's family pieces shine and her choice of color is positively joyful. In the kitchen, a window opens to what Linda's children refer to as "the cozy room." The punchy hues and wonderful art-work create a welcoming space that is typically where people want to gather. The mid-century Polish kilim features an eye-popping atom design.

The warmth and cottage charm of the dining room lends itself to many lingering dinner parties and the barn accommodates over fifty guests for piano recitals. A sublime portrait of Linda's mother, Broadway actress Maggie Mullen, hangs above the buffet. International decor and artifacts abound, and many pieces were gifts from exchange students the family has hosted over the years. Linda's take on vintage is eclectic, inviting, and deeply memorable.

PAGE 60: *The window in Linda's kitchen gives an exciting peek into what her children refer to as "the cozy room." The folk art metal rooster was a gift from one of the many exchange students who stayed with the family over the years.* ABOVE: *Linda's a great hostess and often entertains large groups of people. When the setting is more intimate, however, a proper table is always set with vintage pieces. The Brutalist candelabrum adds an unexpected eclectic touch.*

The portrait of Linda's mother, Maggie, by Henry Strater hangs over the buffet in the dining room. (Another version hangs in the Museum of American Art in Ogunquit, Maine.) I love how she gently placed a rose on the upper right-hand corner. The stone and stucco walls are a wonderfully rugged juxtaposition to elegant subject matter, and the molecular pattern and punchy colors of the mid-century Polish kilim are sensational. FOLLOWING SPREAD: "The cozy room" in all its glory. The confluence of eighteenth-century rustic beams and stone walls with playful mid-century furniture and artwork is pure delight and makes it easy to understand why it's everyone's favorite room in the house. A patron of the arts, Linda knows how to use color and here also showcases several local painters. The joyful cityscape to the far left was done by Linda as a child.

The kilim and artwork really pop in this room and Linda pulled colors from them for the solid sofas. The white walls and table lamps are so subtle that the room is both vibrant and calming at the same time. Linda loves to entertain and uses all of her vintage serving pieces. I particularly love the rainbow of antique American glass finger bowls on the bottom shelf, which Linda makes relevant by using to serve nuts, dip, ice cream, and a multitude of other delights. FOLLOWING SPREAD: The copper pots, molds, and ladles hung above the butcher-block table in Linda's kitchen look like an art installation, but she uses and polishes them regularly. The Bon Appetit trivet is a nod to her Julia Child portrayals, and the mortars and pestles are routinely used to make guacamole and relishes. The framed photo of her father, John Root, whose vision it was to transform the space from dilapidated barn to beautiful home, is always front and center.

chapter four

A FOREVER HOME

*Pat Hamilton's 1850 Ancestral House
with Traditional Vintage Style*

Pat Hamilton knows how to throw a party. Her holiday gatherings are legendary and every other guest I meet is having as wonderful a time as I am. With Christmas caroling around the piano, we're all in the holiday mood. While her electric personality brings us all together, the home provides a warm and wonderful backdrop where mingling is easy.

Pat told me that the home has always been used for parties, and fund-raisers. She and her husband, Bruce, routinely host visiting conductors and musicians from the Riverside Symphony, many of whom are visiting America for the first time. Hospitality is what this home is all about. In fact, Pat believes it has a personality all its own. "This home is a living, breathing thing," she told me.

Built in 1840 for Pat's family, the stately townhome has seen many generations add their imprint. With original details like the slate mantel, chandeliers (originally gas), and plank floors, the home feels quite traditional in its appointments, yet casual in its vibe. Pat and her husband turned the music room into a library to house his collection of more than 3,000 books—but it still has the baby grand piano as its anchor.

Family portraits are carefully placed among vintage botanical lithographs and other artwork. The wallpaper in the dining room is a replica of a design found at the historic Gallier House in New Orleans. Like so many people I love, Pat uses her vintage and antique pieces—many of which are glassware, china, and other entertaining-related items, all kept in a number of lovely cabinets, both built-in and freestanding.

Pat's color palette is rich and warm and her gorgeous family home is truly a piece of living history.

PAGE 70: *Family portraits are rich and plentiful in Pat's home. The warmth of this paneled library is palpable and is even further embellished with an antique Persian rug, family photos, and sentimental heirlooms. The home's original slate mantel is faux-painted to resemble marble.* OPPOSITE: *Pat entertains frequently and, like many of my friends, she uses all of her vintage serving pieces. The cabinet interiors are as well decorated as the home's interiors. This is one of several that contains Pat's many collections.* BELOW: *The "Gallier Diamond" seafoam wallpaper in Pat's dining room is by Brunschwig & Fils. It's a reproduction of an heirloom pattern found in the Gallier House in New Orleans.* FOLLOWING SPREAD: *The living room in Pat's home is both formal and comfortable. The warm yellow walls and simple window treatments make it feel fresh and inviting. Traditional vintage furniture is given a modern feel with fun fabrics and throw pillows.*

The antique crystal chandelier in the dining room casts a warm, flattering light and candles and oil lamps are also always aglow. The framed botanical prints, family furniture, and other accents work as a team to create a space that feels both historic and fresh.

The wood-paneled library contains more than 3,000 books (all belonging to Pat's husband, Bruce). The piano is very much a focal point at parties. Every December, Pat and Bruce gather friends and neighbors at their home for an evening of fun and Christmas caroling, as they have for decades. Everyone is handed a songbook and they gather around the piano to belt out tunes and get in the holiday mood.

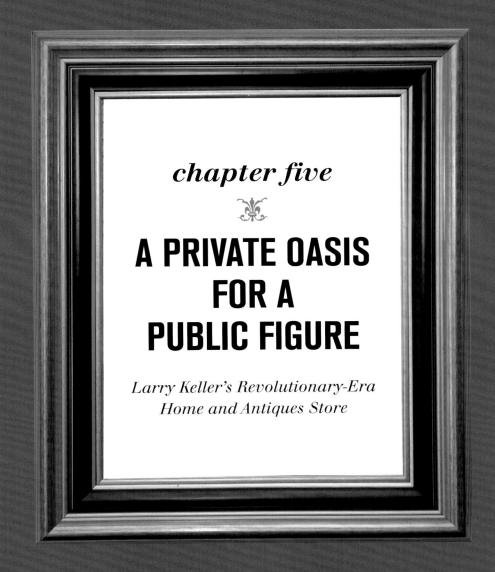

chapter five

A PRIVATE OASIS
FOR A
PUBLIC FIGURE

*Larry Keller's Revolutionary-Era
Home and Antiques Store*

As the mayor of New Hope, Pennsylvania, for more than twenty years, Larry Keller is somewhat of a local celebrity. A patron of the arts, a community volunteer, and a friend to seemingly everyone, Larry is deeply rooted in the community. He's officiated more than eight hundred weddings in the area and has donated the proceeds from that work to the fire company and the rescue squad.

A lifelong native of Bucks County, Larry embarked on his journey as an antiques dealer at age fourteen, when George Hobensack, owner of one of the most venerable shops around, hired him. Hobensack became Larry's mentor throughout high school and college and eventually the two became business partners, forming the antiques store Hobensack & Keller.

After his mentor's passing, Larry purchased the store and the 1760 home on the property where he now resides. There's no sign outside the door, but those in the know are frequent shoppers. And the sea of beautiful garden statuary in front of the driveway often lures in passersby.

While his home is a meticulously curated array of fine art and antiques (many of which have a New Hope provenance), the shop is much more haphazard. Larry makes frequent trips to Europe and combs estate sales and auctions to find pieces with presence and personality. Although new merchandise comes in constantly, the shop retains a comforting feeling of permanence. "Ye Olde Curiosity Shoppe" is a phrase that comes to mind. (Even if Larry jokingly refers to it as looking like the set of *Sanford and Son*, the 1970s TV show.)

How does Larry decide what to keep and what to sell? He says it is much more about the feeling he has for an object, rather than it's financial value. "I can cherish a $300 item and easily live without a $5,000 one. It's all about what you want to see every day. I love my house because when I walk in the door I'm surrounded by the things I love—and I am home."

PAGE 80: *The lush greenery and moss-covered brick of Larry Keller's private garden creates a peaceful background for a few well-chosen pieces of statuary. It's just a hint at what's in store for those who visit his shop.* ABOVE: *Larry's home is filled with paintings by local artists. This piece, done by Mary Sarg in the 1930s, depicts the corner of Main and Bridge Streets in New Hope and has an Edward Hopper feel.* OPPOSITE: *Fine English and European antiques fill Larry's home. There are a multitude of breakfronts, which house his mammoth collection of china.* BELOW: *The details on the jeweled stained glass in Larry's bay window are opulent and joyful.*

LEFT: *The grand archway in Larry's living room is made all the more so by the artful positioning of a massive French vertigris bronze sculpture by Antonin Mercié titled* Gloria Victis. *Hailing from the 1870s, it was at one time France's national symbol, honoring fallen soldiers and offering a hope for recovery as a nation. Another copy of the piece is in the National Gallery of Art in Washington, D.C.* FOLLOWING SPREAD: *The bay window that looks out onto Larry's private garden always feels bright and fresh, even on the grayest day. All the natural light makes it easy to enjoy the extensive art collection.*

With floor-to-ceiling antiques and vintage finds, Larry's store, Hobensack & Keller, feels like a step back in time. Merchandise hails from both local estates and European buying trips. The Broadway sign propped high upon a shelf is fun and speaks to the fact that while close in proximity, New York City feels worlds away.

FOLLOWING SPREAD: *Larry's store certainly has a bit of an English feel, sort of like "Ye Olde Curiosity Shoppe." The layers of silver, artwork, and other treasures are like a time capsule just waiting to be discovered.*

ABOVE: *Art, mirrors, and fine porcelain abound in Larry's store. The shadow box honoring someone's athletic victories long ago is a work of art on its own. There's always a great selection of andirons, which add an instant feeling of history to the hearth of a home.* OPPOSITE: *A sea of hand-hooked antique Persian rugs hang from the large rack, making them easy to peruse. They truly are artwork for the floor.*

chapter five A PRIVATE OASIS FOR A PUBLIC FIGURE

The many faces of Larry's wonderfully curated garden statuary. From gods and saints to world leaders and gargoyles. Even meerkats have their place in the sun. The figure in the upper-right corner is in Larry's personal garden; it's another piece by a local artist, Harry Rosen.

PREVIOUS SPREAD: *The maze of garden statuary lures in many a passerby to Hobensack & Keller. These outdoor ornaments are the hallmark of the store. Every imaginable creation is in stock at any given time.*

chapter five **A PRIVATE OASIS FOR A PUBLIC FIGURE**

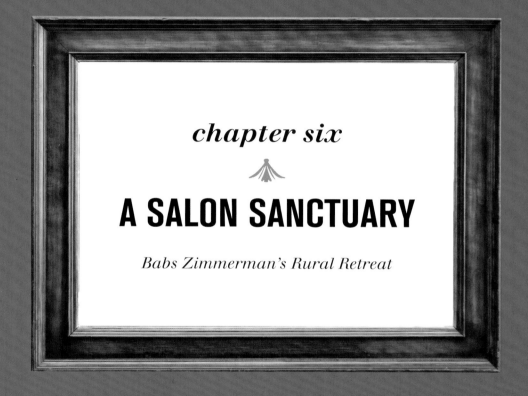

chapter six

A SALON SANCTUARY

Babs Zimmerman's Rural Retreat

Potter, sculptor, rug maker, and humanitarian Babs Zimmerman has a quiet strength that she brings to all she does. Babs's rural home effortlessly showcases her work and her collections. Her use of pattern and color is expert and her eye for detail is outstanding.

A native of Bucks County, Babs had no intention of becoming a lifelong resident, yet while on her honeymoon in 1968, her mother wrote her about an old house for sale in the area and the seed was planted. In a moment of synchronicity, upon their return, Babs and her husband, Paul, (a screenwriter known for *The King of Comedy*) decided to look at houses on a whim. The very house her mother wrote her about was the second one they saw and they bought it immediately.

Built in 1860, the home showcases period details including star motif moldings, leaded glass windows, chandeliers, and original doors, and plank flooring. On a rafter in the basement, Babs found a "Grant for President" campaign button. But the traces of history don't stop there. Her son Ian found a Revolutionary War cannonball in the backyard that led the family to do some research that revealed their property was used as the staging ground for the Battle of Trenton.

Babs says her design sensibility was greatly influenced by her mentor, Lenore Marshall, a poet and longtime peace and anti-nuclear activist, who also had exquisite taste. Most things have been bought at flea markets or local auctions. The living room is relatively small but made to look larger with the use of different shades of blue (Babs's favorite color). The wallpaper in the hallway is a William Morris design; the wallpaper in the dining room is a copy of a remnant that was found in an old trunk.

Babs's late husband was a francophile so the couple collected Quimper china (relatively inexpensive and wonderfully decorative). "Most people think if you pay a lot for something it's valuable, but I've found this is not always the case. I can get immense pleasure from a slightly cracked plate I bought for a dollar at a flea market."

I'm certainly not the only one who loves visiting this inviting home. Babs's list of houseguests is a veritable "who's who" running the gamut from Blythe Danner to Abbie Hoffman to Monty Python alums Michael Palin and Terry Jones.

PAGE 98: *For a house so rich in American history, it seems natural for the palette of Babs's home to include some red, white, and blue. In her case, however, it's more like cinnamon, cream, and cornflower—a warm and wonderful combination that plays out in a variety of rugs, wallpapers, fabrics, art, and pottery.* ABOVE: *The framed photo in the center captures a sweet moment between Babs's son Ian and the family's Norwegian au pair Hanne. The other wonderfully eclectic pieces are mostly flea market finds.* OPPOSITE: *The day we photographed, Babs was picking daffodils from her garden, which she placed in art pottery vases all over the house. (She was also kind enough to give a bunch to me!) She created the bust that sits atop the large antique dresser in the entryway. The painting above is a portrait of her son Ian done by Joby Baker.*

PREVIOUS SPREAD: *The living room is bright and sunny and the perfect place to read or gather with friends. When it's her turn, this is where Babs hosts our play-reading club. The home's original mantel has wonderful star motifs atop its columns; the Picasso above it was purchased by Babs and her late husband, Paul, when they were on their honeymoon.*
RIGHT: *The original staircase, molding, and other woodwork details underscore the home's historic roots. Babs's use of playful patterns is inspiring. The wallpaper in the staircase is by William Morris and the wallpaper in the dining room beyond was based on a pattern found in an old trunk. Many of the fabrics evoke a woodland—almost a fairy tale theme.*

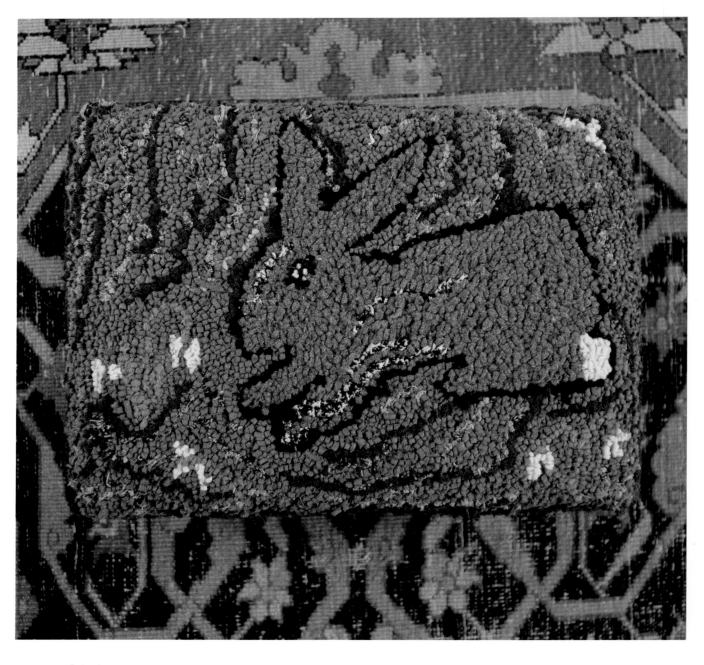

ABOVE: *Babs's hooked rug seat covers and pillows are all over the house. First she draws a subject freehand on paper, then she transfers it to canvas, selects the colors, and begins hooking, an art she learned on a visit to Nova Scotia. This rabbit covers a footstool near the living room fireplace.* OPPOSITE: *Another view of the living room showcases Babs's artful eye for mixing pattern and color. A pottery angel she created watches over the room.*

At the dining table, Babs is known for creating joyful, creative tablescapes. Mixing candleholders she created in her pottery studio along with silver counterparts she found at various flea markets, the result is always welcoming and fun. The silver creamer filled with spoons is a clever touch when entertaining a number of people—it feels a bit like a bouquet. FOLLOWING SPREAD: In the kitchen, Babs features a wall collage of plates and tiles she and her husband collected over the years. Most are French (Quimper) but others include a Danish trio by Bjørn Winblad, and an Italian plate featuring a bat in full flight (a gift from her dear friend Lelia). The Russian painting was a flea market find and Babs promises that one day she'll make a hooked rug in its likeness.

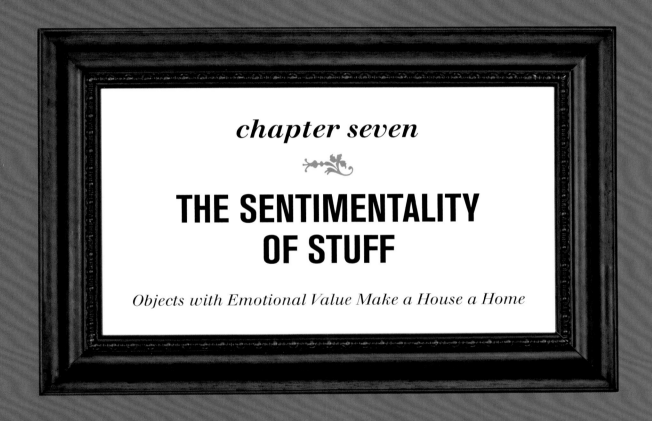

chapter seven

THE SENTIMENTALITY OF STUFF

Objects with Emotional Value Make a House a Home

I'm proudly sentimental. In fact, a visit to my home is a bit of a sentimental journey for my friends and relatives as it's full of art, furniture, and objects that have personal history for us. For visitors who don't know me well, these pieces provide a surefire way to get acquainted. While items with emotional value are all over my home and this book, this chapter highlights a few of my favorites.

Financial value may have its place, but it's the emotional value of objects that makes a house a home. I always say if you want to know people, ask them about their stuff. This is where the three C's of *Vintage Living* come into play. All sentimentally valuable items bring comfort, connection, and continuity to our homes and our daily lives. When we share them with friends and loved ones, we share part of ourselves.

Sentimental home furnishings are typically family pieces, or items that remind us of a time or place, including photos of people we love and, in many cases, letters or notes or other ephemeral items that conjure up happy memories.

There are some who say photos belong in albums, but I wholeheartedly disagree. I love seeing framed photographs in a home and I proudly display mine all over the house. I like grouping them and have arranged many on two tables in the entryway that belonged to my grandmother. I also enjoy tucking the wonderful notes I've received from my grandmother and other loved ones in spots around the house.

Some of the things that mean the most to us are ones that were made by those we love. For me these are things like the sampler that hangs in my dining room. It was stitched and framed for me by my sister Robin when I moved to New York to go to New York University. The phrase along the bottom has rung true for me always: "For Those Who Have Faith, No Explanation is Necessary. For Those Who Don't, None is Possible."

PAGE 112: *My friends Max and Anita, who also live in a historic home and love shopping at flea markets, found this RCA Victor radio on a particularly memorable day thrifting together. They thought they'd bring it home for some decorative appeal in their dining room. Much to their surprise, when they plugged it in, it worked perfectly. Now it's often on in the background. Their cat Rumi thinks it's pretty purrfect.* ABOVE, LEFT: *My grandfather opened our family's interior design business in 1936. I keep one of his cards next to mine on a side table in my dressing room.* ABOVE, RIGHT: *I wrote my first book when I was nine, all about my favorite movie stars (Katharine Hepburn, Cary Grant, Judy Holliday, Vivien Leigh, to name a few). It began as a class project and took on a life of its own. It's always on a table somewhere in my home.* BELOW: *A sampling of the sampler my sister Robin stitched for me, with that wonderful wisdom.* OPPOSITE: *My dear friends Lelia and Paul Matthews have a home filled with objects that hold great emotional value. Paul painted this portrait of Lelia when she was pregnant with the first of their four children. It captures the mood and beautiful moment perfectly and has hung in their living room for decades.* FOLLOWING SPREAD: *Lelia's mother's diary lies open on the coffee table and reading a passage, or even seeing the handwriting, is an instant connection to her. I love how the photos of Paul and Lelia's children are not propped, but lie flat around the diary. It all feels so personal and very dear.*

FOR THOSE WHO HAVE FAITH
NO EXPLANATION IS NECESSARY
FOR THOSE WHO DON'T NONE IS POSSIBLE

sits in all her pure white splendor
w the hall at Severnsea — The
chief events on the way to Capetown
were crossing the equator — for the first time
all of us who were doing so, ordered
to do something — I did Rennell
Island — a Hula Hula dance — and
waking one afternoon to smell a
horrible smell — The whole sea
covered with oil where an Italian
tanker had been torpedoed the
night before — And the Cape Swells —
As we approached Capetown there
were huge ocean swells. We were
ordered off the decks + all our
belongings and to close and lock
all doors and ports — The Captain
asked me to the Bridge — and
what a sight — The huge swell
broke over the ship like Niagara
Falls with only the Bridge above
water — !!! After we left Capetown
we had one Dramatic experience —
Just at dusk a ship appeared —

Friday, April 17

Saturday, April 18

Sunday, April 19

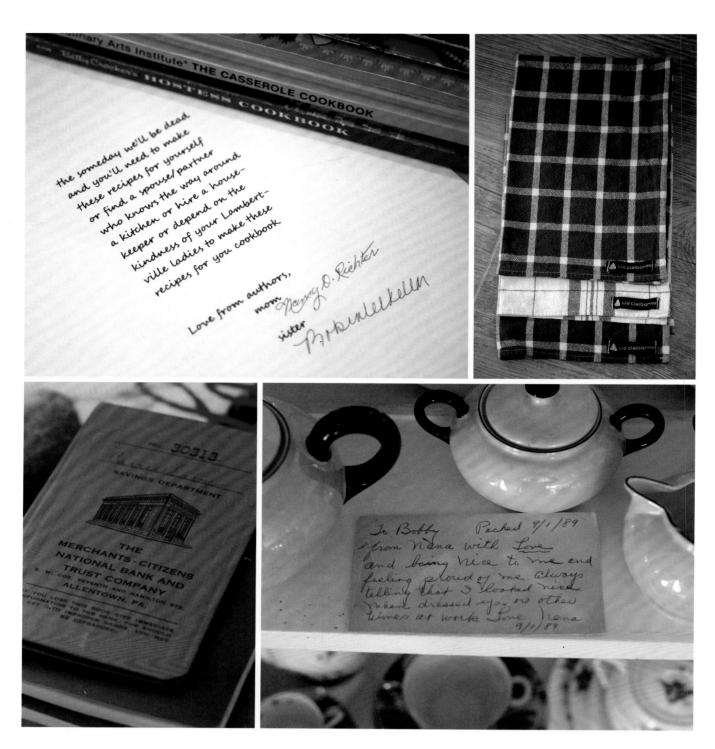

My mom and sister created a family cookbook as a present and I love the dedication. My brother made these tea towels for my sister when he was working at Liz Claiborne in the 1980s and she passed them along to me when I moved into my house. My grandmother's bankbook has great emotional value and I keep it on the same table with my grandfather's business card. Displayed with my grandmother's tea set is the note she wrote me when she gave it to me—it's part of its history. These ephemeral objects are personal and dear.

chapter eight

❧

MORE IS MORE: LIVING WITH COLLECTIONS

I don't have "a" collection, I have collections . . . in fact, I have too many collections to count. They include art deco china, modern glassware, pottery, and furniture from the 1940s. And I do believe the best way to treat a collection is to make it (every one of them!) the star of the room.

For example, I designed my kitchen around the vintage china I inherited from an antiques dealer mentor and friend. I featured the china in plain glass front cabinetry, which I lit from overhead, so I could enjoy it every day. I took my cues from the colors of the china (orange, blue, green, and yellow) and picked out complementary appliances and design elements like an orange fridge and green countertops, which helped the space feel harmonious.

If your stuff is going to be the focus of your home, keep the paint and furnishings simple. I also suggest unifying displays by color. I have a dresser top in my bedroom that is covered with pottery, but it is in varying shades of orange so it is automatically easy on the eye.

The easiest solution to an out-of-hand collection is to recognize that you don't have to have all of your stuff on display at once. You can rotate your collections according to the seasons, or simply as you wish. Arrange your collection so it brings happiness and remember, your stuff is what makes a house a home. But if you find your collections are getting out of hand, you might want to consider selling off pieces and using the profits to buy items of an even better caliber.

Whether it's foo dogs, porcelain boxes, or tin lunch boxes, collections can take on a life of their own. When decorating with them, I do believe there is power in numbers. But how do you know when you've jumped the shark? I think it's a very personal decision.

What I can offer as a guide are a few of my basic design principles when it comes to living with collections:

1. Color Block

When you arrange anything by color it harmonizes the objects and is more pleasing to the eye. This might mean assembling things of all one color or choosing just a few colors to display.

2. Aim for Symmetry/Balance

When you have many objects, assembling them in a way that looks orderly automatically gives everything a sense of unity. Often the display becomes more about the final, collective look than about any individual object.

3. Lighting Is Everything

To create importance around a collection, I encourage special lighting to showcase it as a whole and in some cases to highlight some of the most prized pieces.

PAGE 122: *People typically spend a long time in my bathroom, not because of nature calling, but because they enjoy taking in my collection of WWII posters, statues, toys, and more. Bathrooms are great places to display collections and show your sense of humor.* ABOVE: *My friends Max and Anita had this special shelf built with back lighting to display their collection of white American art pottery. The ambient light and pleasing arrangement is a perfect accent in their dining room.* BELOW: *My china collection is massive and I enjoy using it on a daily basis. As a result, I consider the inside of my cabinets a canvas for displaying them. Color blocking helps even the most haphazard display feel harmonious.* OPPOSITE: *When I found these arrows in an old barn, I thought the colors were wonderful and that they resembled a bouquet of wildflowers. Placing them in a vase is a fun way to enjoy them all year round.*

ABOVE: *Vintage action figures and toys (like the Lone Ranger and Tonto) are playfully assembled in my powder room. Here they are on a windowsill surrounding an old bank sign.* BELOW: *Ceramic, chalkware, and cardboard soldiers, sailors, and marines join Uncle Sam and other patriotic figures in my bathroom. They surround an art deco medicine cabinet and sit atop a vintage wicker table that used to be in the entryway of our family business.*

Details of some of my favorite patriotic figures in my bathroom. The art deco magazine rack is a favorite piece and holds copies of the war-era magazine Air News.

TOP: *Once upon a time people could answer an ad in a magazine and have a photo of their loved one turned into something called a "Humanette." Similar to paper dolls, each was mounted on board and freestanding. My collection of them resides in the guest room.* BOTTOM LEFT: *This whimsical pairing of mother doe and baby squirrel sit on a windowsill in my kitchen along with other pieces in my fun figural collection. I consider them a blended family.* BOTTOM RIGHT: *Bob's Big Boy is a favorite brand icon of mine for obvious reasons. This rubber version sits atop a vintage canister along with a bisque gnome resting on an old can of beets (actual beets are long gone) on my kitchen counter.* OPPOSITE: *This small English corner cupboard in my TV room holds whatever books I'm currently enjoying along with vintage canisters, art pottery, and favorite family pieces. The Russian circus bear bookends belonged to my friend Sunny and the cardinal belonged to my grandmother. The bisque bunny band resides here year round, except during Easter.*

EDGEMONT
CRACKERS

A. JAVANESA

RUA do ARSENAL 102
TEL. 22722

Flea Market Secrets Jonty Hearnden

R.D.Laing knots

Ask and It Is Given Esther and Jerry Hicks

DARING GREATLY BRENÉ BROWN, Ph.D.,L.M.S.W.

JEN SINCERO YOU ARE A BADASS AT MAKING MONEY

KENT NERBURN Small Graces

KENT NERBURN THE HIDDEN BEAUTY OF EVERYDAY LIFE

KENT NERBURN Simple Truths

Notes from the Universe

JOSEPH CAMPBELL THE POWER OF MYTH WITH BILL MOYERS

FRENCH WAYS AND THEIR MEANING EDITH WHARTON

Markets of Paris DIXON LONG & MARJORIE R. WILLIAMS

SOLDIERS THREE KIPLING

A Concise History of Modern Painting Herbert Read PRAEGER

THE MERRY MAKER YOUNG FOLKS LIBRARY

WRITING the MEMOIR ● From Truth to Art

Lindenberger The 50s & 60s Kitchen Schiffer

OPPOSITE: *The round table in my dressing room holds coins, sunglasses, and the usual items that are emptied from my pockets in the evening. My blended version of the Three Kings, with each from different flea markets.* TOP: *A collection of stone and papier-mâché pears on a side table in my friend Tom's home.* BOTTOM: *This resin hand was likely someone's art project at one point. I found it at a flea market and thought it would be an excellent way to display my collection of big rings.*

ABOVE: *Next to her kitchen sink, Babs has displayed a wonderful collection of cocoa, tea, and coffee canisters from her travels. The graphics are wonderful. They are the perfect example of how pieces take on a whole new life when arranged together.* OPPOSITE: *This early painted hutch in the kitchen is filled with Quimper and other pieces of French pottery, all of which is used on a regular basis. The informality of its display is refreshing and feels like an ever-changing art installation.*

Sometimes shopping vintage venues is a great way to find inspiration on how to display a collection. This vintage dress form at the Philly Flea takes on a new life as a base to showcase vintage buttons. The row of macramé plant holders at the People's Store in Lambertville, New Jersey, is a fun way to display a collection of glass vases. In both cases, somewhat ordinary objects are elevated for decorative appeal. FOLLOWING SPREAD: *My kitchen cabinets are filled with colorful collections of vintage china. This set of Riviera by Homer Laughlin has great colors and art deco lines. My friend Sunny gave it to me and I referred to the colors for inspiration when designing my New York City kitchen.*

chapter nine

✳

ENTERTAINING

Bringing People Together

Modern technology is amazing and I embrace most of it—especially the wonders of social media. How incredible is it to connect with people all over the world with a few taps on your cell phone? The only problem, I find, is that when I'm so busy connecting on various platforms, I'm not present in the actual moment. Now more than ever, I find vintage objects allow us to be more present and social with each other. I routinely host and attend dinner parties where no one has their phones out for the duration of the evening. Hours go by with conversation, connectivity, laughter, and dining. No one is forced to keep their technology out of the picture; it just happens organically as the vintage vibe begins to take over.

Bringing that vibe to any gathering is easy and fun. There are many other ways to entertain with vintage items. I particularly enjoy serving with vintage china and linens; I even often use place cards and send out actual invitations. And don't forget vintage aprons (I often gift them to friends).

My dear friend Lelia frequently uses her mother's serving ware. The pieces are quite ornate and special and always spark conversation. Her home is beautiful, yet informal, and she uses these vintage pieces in a more casual way than they were used a century ago. The point is that she still uses them and makes them relevant.

Vintage cookbooks offer up old recipes that could be long forgotten but might soon become new favorites. I recently found a vintage recipe box with someone's old recipes written inside.

Talk about a life story told through food! I picked up the little box because I thought it would look cute in my kitchen, but what I discovered inside was priceless. There are countless entertaining guides and cookbooks out there from the 1920s through the '80s. Pick one up and tap some of the ideas.

Vintage board games often spark memories and evoke lots of laughter. Monopoly, Chinese checkers, and those great board games inspired by our favorite TV shows all make for a fun evening. I also have a '30s fortune-telling game that people love.

While you're busy dining, conversing, and/or playing a board game, don't forget about vintage music. My stereo is regularly humming with vinyl and I happily take requests. Guests enjoy the process of taking out an album, placing it on the turntable, flicking the switch, and watching the needle drop. All of this helps us be a bit more mindful than a digital playlist does. My vintage TV set is also a crowd pleaser. Classic TV shows and films have always been a big part of my life and sharing them with others is a wonderful way to connect. *The Mary Tyler Moore Show* is one of my favorites to watch on a Saturday night (when it originally aired). Mary made it cool to stay home on a Saturday night—and she still does!

Even if you're not literally using vintage items, you can entertain in a vintage way . . . either by gathering around a piano and singing (with vintage or new sheet music), having a limbo contest (so fun!), or simply holding a flashlight under your chin and telling ghost stories—to name just a few examples!

A TREASURY of PLAY IDEAS for TOTS

FUNNY MOUSTACHE

...ials:

Paper
Black crayon
Cord

...e bottom of this page, you will see the pattern of a really ...moustache. Copy it or trace it onto a piece of white paper. ...and black. Now cut it out. Poke two small holes in it as ...attern.

...d through the holes. Now place the ...and tie the cord around his ... ...and out beautif...

PAGE 138: *When people visit my home they all want to gather around the 1950 RCA Victor TV in my living room. My good friends at Vintage Vibe in Doylestown reconditioned it so that it plays DVDs and is cable ready. The case and stand retain their original integrity and, thanks to my clever friends, it works perfectly.* OPPOSITE: *Having a party? Use vintage invitations! They are out there online and at flea markets. These belong to my friends Greg and Joe, whose entertaining style begins with invitations and plays out out with vintage china and old-fashioned recipes.* LEFT: *There are millions of vintage kids party books out there. They showcase ideas for having a good time before digital devices came along. How fun is it to invite children (and/or the child in all of us) to have fun with only paper, crayons, and some string?* BELOW: *Don't forget about puzzles. They are a fun way to interact, slow down, be mindful, and feel connected.*

TOP: *Vintage cookbooks are in plentiful supply at flea markets. They are a great way to reconnect with dishes you may recall from your childhood or discover heritage recipes that might just become new favorites. As an added bonus, many vintage recipes use fewer ingredients and are less complicated than ones that are out there today.* BOTTOM: *Breakfast in bed is a very vintage and wonderful way to treat a special guest—or to pamper yourself. Especially in the winter months, I like to cozy up with the newspaper, a pot of coffee, and a treat or two. Using favorite china makes it all the more enjoyable.* OPPOSITE: *At one time every kitchen had a recipe box. Mine still does. In fact, I have several—one with family favorites that's priceless to me. I found this one at a thrift store and felt like I had to give it a home. Luckily it turns out to hold some great recipes.*

chapter nine ENTERTAINING

Strawberry Ice-Cream Pie

Cake Fillings

Beverages

Pickles-Relish

Vegetables
Fritters

Biscuits-Bread

Preserves

Frostings
Cake-Cookies

Tuna Casserole

in.   1 can condensed cream of mushroom soup

⅓ c milk

1 - 6½ oz 7 oz can, tuna

Chocolate Fudge

2 squares chocolate   ¾ cup water
   (or ½ cup cocoa)   1 tablespoon light corn syrup
2 cups sugar   ¼ teaspoon salt
½ cup evaporated milk   2 tablespoons butter
   (or 1 cup fresh milk   1 teaspoon vanilla
   and omit water)   ½ cup broken nut meats

ABOVE: *Vinyl is back in a big way. As a result, every big box store is selling record players. That said, none sound as beautifully resonant as a wooden stereo. I found mine at a yard sale for $10 in 1998. It's a 1954 RCA Orthophonic and when it's on you can hear it all over the house. Recently I found another great specimen and traded the dealer a mid-century chair for it. I've spied many others at flea markets and antiques shops all over. Since every home used to have one, they are out there for the finding!* OPPOSITE: *I inherited my family's records and am always adding to my collection. Playing vintage vinyl is a fun way to relax and connect with friends. I put on a stack of ten records and let my RCA do the rest.*

JOAN BAEZ
DIAMONDS & RUST
JOHN DENVER'S GREATEST HITS
Peter Paul and Mary
IN THE WIND
WARNER BROS. RECORDS
1507

Vintage games often open up a floodgate of memories as many people grew up playing them. I love a good game night and have many fun evenings with friends playing board games. These carpet bowls were not in my home growing up, but I still love them. Most vintage games and boards are visually appealing, some are even hand-made, and add a decorative touch to a coffee table.

chapter ten

HAPPY HOLIDAYS

*Conjuring and Creating
Your Own Happy
Memories Together*

Most people who know me know that Christmas is a pretty big deal in my world. I love all of the vintage ornaments, lights and decorations, cards, wrapping, and more. But while Christmas certainly remains my favorite holiday, I enjoy and celebrate all of them with vintage déecor and traditions.

One of the reasons I think holidays are so important is that they help us to connect and share memories while creating new ones. Vintage holiday items are out there in plentiful supply because everyone owned them. As such, so many of us have sentimental attachments to these treasured pieces.

That Halloween cardboard cutout you remember hanging on your aunt's kitchen wall every year? You might find its counterpart at a flea market, and it will bring back many fond memories. The same goes for Christmas décor. I know many people who treasure family tree ornaments, and I include myself in that camp. However, as we all know, sometimes family heirlooms break or get lost. Luckily, when that happens you can often find its counterpart at a vintage venue and still keep those memories alive.

What I love about vintage holiday decor is that certain pieces can evoke long-forgotten memories. Whenever I see certain Halloween items, for instance, I think of my brother Johnny. One year for Halloween he came home from college

to take me trick-or-treating. I'd been wearing my homemade costume all day at school and it had basically fallen apart. He came to the rescue by giving me his plaid woolen coat and hat and a small ax he grabbed from the basement. "You're a woodsman," he declared. And so I was. It was the best Halloween ever and probably has a lot to do with why I pretty much dress the same way today.

Our memories are wrapped up in these objects and at the holidays we get to open them and share them. How great is that?

PAGE 150: *My favorite vintage Halloween cutouts are cuter than they are spooky. When I was growing up, my mom had similar ones she hung on our kitchen wall every year.* ABOVE: *A trio of choirboy candles that sat on my grandmother's buffet every Christmas for decades. Now they live on a side table in my living room near a photo of her. I can't pass by them without smiling.* OPPOSITE: *A reflection of the tabletop tree in my sitting room and a glimpse of the large tree in the living room beyond. Since they're living things and bring so much joy, it seems fitting to name my trees. I call these Betty and Mary, after two of the sisters who once lived in my house. When I first toured the house, this is what I envisioned. Where the Christmas trees are going to go is a big deal for me!* BELOW: *Joyful garlands of glass beads and Tibetan prayer flags adorn Linda Kenyon's floor-to-ceiling Christmas tree.*

Christmas

Christmas, in my humble opinion, really is the most wonderful time of the year. I've always thought so and likely always will. The anticipation, preparation, shopping, and gift giving are all things that bring me comfort and joy. Of course it's the decorating part that really gets my jingle bells ringing. Even as a kid I had at least three trees. Now I'm up to about twenty—and counting.

One of the most marvelous things about vintage Christmas decorations is that they evoke so many memories. Bringing them out every year is kind of like visiting old friends. I started collecting Christmas ornaments when I was seven. By the time I was ten, I had a nine-foot tree decked out in vintage and it just snowballed from there.

I love sharing my trees with family and friends and seeing their reactions as my vintage decor brings back memories of their Christmases past. Before you know it, we're all talking about a time and place that is long gone, but is very real in that moment. Sharing those things is one of the most magical aspects of Christmas. If my decorating helps get people there, I consider it an honor.

While some vintage Christmas decor has become quite pricey, it's the emotional value of it all that really matters. Some of my most treasured Christmas finds don't hold a great deal of financial value, but they're priceless to me— like my grandmother's trio of choirboy candles, the stockings my brother made, the snow globe my sister gave me, and vintage ornaments that belonged to my mom and both grandmothers. While my collection is large and ever-growing, these pieces have the greatest meaning to me.

ABOVE: *Stockings my brother made us one Christmas always evoke wonderful memories. Now they hang in my home (I tie them to the balusters on the staircase with fishing line). Naturally, I put an orange in the toe before adding the gifts just like Mom did for us.* OPPOSITE: *My dining room has a festive tablecloth my sister made for me from vintage fabric I found at the flea market. The center bowl and candleholders belonged to my grandmother.* FOLLOWING SPREAD: *My living room is the heart of my Christmas holiday decorating. All my live trees are delivered by Bountiful Acres, the local gem of a Christmas tree farm. I pick them out and have them delivered the day after Thanksgiving. And then the fun begins. This nine-foot tree holds the majority of my family ornaments and many others that have special meaning.*

OPPOSITE: *The patriotic tree in my bathroom is simply decked with American-made war-era ornaments in red, white, and blue. Around the base I draped a star-spangled satin drapery panel I found at a flea market. Since the room is already decorated with WWII items, this tree is right at home . . . and consequently it's the one I leave up the longest!* ABOVE: *A few of my tabletop trees: the early feather tree is decorated with antique German ornaments. The flocked tree is decorated with vintage red balls I found in their original boxes. The white tree is decked with some of the first American-made ornaments—I love they way they look as an ensemble; one of my "Velveteen Rabbit" trees features some of the oldest ornaments in my collection.*

This is one of my "Velveteen Rabbit" trees, so called because their ornaments once had bright colors, but time and age wore them away. Since these antique blown glass ornaments are silvered on the inside, they become beautiful and luminescent in an entirely different way. I see the beauty in age, and this tree is a favorite for its look and metaphor.

This whimsical mid-century holiday display was someone's DIY project many years ago. I found it at a flea market and thought it had the right mix of kitsch and presence. On the windowsill in my powder room it takes on a rather magical glow.

It's fun to get lost in the branches of a Christmas tree and appreciate each ornament. While it's impossible to name favorites, these are a sweet sampling: a close-up glimpse at a nook of the Velveteen Rabbit tree; my grandmother's Father Christmas; a wonderful, rare Italian Alps ornament; and a Fabergé-style egg.

More sweet decorations: an ornament given to me by the people who sold me the house—it spent many Christmases here and now it will spend even more; one of my grandmother's bird clothespins I use on the kitchen tree; a wintry Father Christmas; and a large fanciful mushroom.

LEFT: *The kitchen tree is always a favorite. I use vintage ornaments that pull from the colors of the room. They include American-made ornaments from the tail end of WWII. Since resources were rationed, they are plain glass balls with no silvering or metal caps. The brightly painted colors make them joyful. I added my grandmother's parakeet clothespins and handmade paper Moravian Star ornaments and wrapped a vintage tablecloth that used to cover our picnic table every year around the base. Underneath are some of my favorite vintage holiday baubles. I named this tree Dessie, after the youngest sister who grew up in my house.* ABOVE: *Milk and cookies for Santa look especially inviting when paired with a vintage plate and tumbler.*

DRIPPINGS

OPPOSITE: *The company that made this 1940s nativity set also made action figures like the Lone Ranger and Superman. The colors are so fun I displayed them in the kitchen with two vintage trays. My take on vintage is that things don't have to be used or displayed as they originally were—in fact, being creative is half the fun of decorating with them.* ABOVE: *The sweet vintage Christmas tree nightlight sits atop a repurposed kitchen range light and timer. It's flanked by my favorite celluloid and papier-mâché santa and snowman.* FOLLOWING SPREAD: *The entrance to my living room and sitting room, all decked out for the holiday. Hanging between the pocket doors is a large ribbed art deco ornament in a wonderful champagne hue, which was likely a store display. On the 1954 RCA Victor, the yule log crackles while familiar carols play.*

A 1930s wax German celestial tree topper sits atop a plateau I covered with cobalt and clear wire-wrapped balls. The star tins used to hold typewriter ribbon. The center bowl in the dining room holds red and green vintage balls in various sizes. The white nativity was made by a friend's mother many moons ago in a ceramics class.

This tree of jolly Santas was likely made as a store display. Here they're making merry in front of a display of boxes that once held artificial snow. Under the tree I display boxes and vintage wrapping from old department stores. The little mid-century elves feel right at home snuggled in a bowl of clementines.

Linda Kenyon's home is warm and wonderful all year round, and at Christmas it is especially so. The twenty-four-foot tree is magical and as eclectic as it is grand. Ornaments hail from all over the globe and many have deeply rooted family connections. Linda's father was a set decorator on The Perry Como Show *and many of those wonderful ornaments, including garlands of multicolored glass beads, now adorn the bows of this majestic evergreen.*

Valentine's Day

February 14th is the day we celebrate love and the greeting card companies have been helping us do so for more than 150 years. As a result, there are lots of vintage valentines out there at flea markets and antiques markets. I shop for them all year long and enjoy giving them to friends and loved ones at this time of the year. Truth be told, vintage cards are typically less expensive than their new counterparts and are often works of art.

To personalize them, I simply take double-sided tape and affix each one to new card stock, or sometimes to a heart-shaped box of chocolates (if I really like you!). I also enjoy hunting for heart-shaped jewelry and trinket boxes, which I then display along with vintage cards in different spots around the house. Many cards I find were given by children to one another at school. I tend to like those the best. They are a sweet reminder that love is not always romantic and that Valentine's Day is meant to celebrate and spread love to everyone.

ABOVE: *Valentine's cards as found at a flea market. Like most holiday items, I buy them off-season when they're bargains. They are fun to decorate with and to gift. Some are even frame-worthy.* OPPOSITE: *My grandmother tatted these adorable little baskets when she was a young girl living on a farm in Topton, Pennsylvania. These have great emotional value and I place small candies and favors in them on Valentine's Day, as well as on Easter and Christmas. To help keep their shape when stored, she always kept them around two old prescription bottles.* FOLLOWING SPREAD: *A new box of Valentine's chocolates gets a vintage twist with a Victorian cut-out card affixed to the front. Well-worn heart-shaped boxes remind me that some of the most loving hearts have been through the mill. An array of sweet Valentine's cards from many eras is always a fun and easy way to decorate for the holiday.*

Easter

Spring always feels like a bit of a miracle after a long winter in the northeast where I live. As such, Easter really is a time to celebrate awakenings—spiritually, physically, and environmentally. It's a chance to be outside, watch things bloom, and celebrate longer light-filled days. Of course as a kid I dyed eggs and enjoyed my fair share of Easter candy. My all-time favorites are peanut butter Rice Krispies chocolate eggs that Mom made every year.

Family dinner was always a big deal with Mom's famous German potato salad and pineapple filling. For me, however, the best part of Easter is the decorating. When I learned that I could have an Easter tree, all bets were off. I've had many over the years in all shapes and sizes and genres.

My most favorite to date is the one featured here. I found it at our local fire company flea market and paid just one dollar. It's a sweet feather tree that's newer but very vintage in its vibe. To decorate it I found hand-painted miniature German wooden egg ornaments at one of my favorite shops, Antique Haven in Kintnersville, Pennsylvania. The marriage of the tree and the eggs is most certainly a happy one!

ABOVE: *This floppy-eared ceramic bunny takes up residence on my kitchen island in front of an old candy store sign.* OPPOSITE: *My new favorite Easter tree with vintage German hand-painted wooden eggs. I love how it joyfully plays with my kitchen curtains.*

Purpose is
what gives life
meaning

LOUIS F. DOW CO.

SUN   APR

1

OPPOSITE: *On my kitchen island I display a vintage cardboard bunny in a very snappy outfit, a papier-mâché duck, and my mom's famous chocolate-dipped peanut butter Rice Krispies eggs.* ABOVE: *I found this anthromorphic chick band in its original box at one of my favorite antiques shops—I think they're a real hoot; a vintage Easter card tucked here and there adds an easy touch of decor to unexpected places; a bright orange ceramic bunny sits atop my vintage French salt box all year long, but at this time of the year he joins in on the fun.*

Halloween

After Christmas, Halloween is my favorite holiday. I have very fond memories of trick-or-treating, homemade costumes, and family time. Because of how Halloween was celebrated in my family, I never thought of it as spooky, but rather as a time for cute, somewhat sassy decorations to make their annual appearance in our home. As an adult I treat it much the same way. While I don't decorate as elaborately for Halloween as I do for Christmas, I do pepper pieces throughout the kitchen and dining room.

Black and orange tend to be the signature palette for the holiday and as such, my vintage pieces really pop. Cardboard cutouts, candles, candy containers, and light-up figures are just a sampling of the sort of decor I hunt for at flea markets all year long. One of my favorite recent finds is a light-up ceramic jack o' lantern made by the same company who made all of those ceramic Christmas trees everyone used to own. Like most great vintage holiday items, I found him off-season (in May) and paid very little. He makes a spooky sweet impact and reminds me of a similar one we had growing up.

Where I live we get massive amounts of trick-or-treaters and for me that is the real celebration of Halloween. My friends Sharon and Sam are wildly talented artists and they outfit me in amazing handmade costumes, which really adds to the fun. We take turns doling out candy to a seemingly endless stream of kids and their parents who are all enjoying a night of fun and festivities. Seeing them in their costumes is such a treat and it takes me back to my own childhood and all the memories I have of the holiday. It feels like things have come full circle.

ABOVE AND OPPOSITE: *A vintage owl candle perches atop a folk-art henhouse on my kitchen counter; a 1930s place card and party favors; the small buffet in my dining room features my new favorite light-up ceramic jack o' lantern and a 1940s cardboard cat; I love how they look in this low, ambient light. Very Halloween-y!* FOLLOWING SPREAD: *The island in my kitchen always serves as a palette for holiday decorating. At Halloween I feature cardboard cutouts, a kooky German candy container, and a few figural candles. How cute are those little jack o' lanterns with wizard hats?*

FRI OCT

31

Difficulties spur us whenever they do
not check us.
—Roede

TO-DAY CANDID CALENDAR

LOUIS F. DOW CO
Goodwill Advertising

SAINT PAUL   MINNESOTA

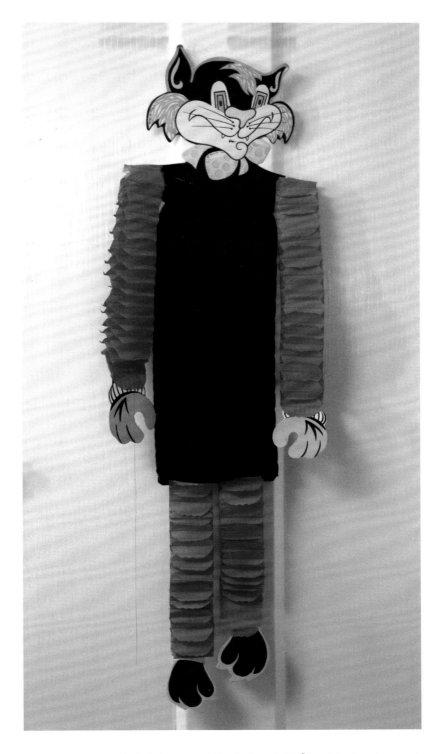

OPPOSITE: *This pair of owl cutouts came from a dealer friend of mine who specializes in vintage holiday decor. I love how the one on the top is winking. They are playfully arranged to be peering over the dining room table.* ABOVE: *My pal Ralph found this cool cat for me. I love the combination of cardboard and crepe paper. This is one of my newest vintage pieces, likely hailing from the late 1960s to the early 1970s. He's so evocative of that time with just a hint of psychedelic influence around his eyes.*

Thanksgiving

Any holiday centering around gratitude and good food is great in my book. For me Thanksgiving is about a meal with my family with all of my favorite things. I've traveled far and wide and have yet to taste stuffing as good as my mom's. Her corn soufflé and pumpkin pie are also dynamite. Of course we use the same beautiful bowl we use for the lima beans every year, and most recently we've begun using my grandmother's china ("Desert Rose" by Franciscan), which brings back memories and connects us to so many happy Thanksgivings past.

Saying a special Thanksgiving prayer and going around the table and expressing what we're thankful for are annual traditions. Admittedly sometimes I have to cut myself off as the food is getting cold. Another tradition is to watch the original *Miracle on 34th Street*. Because the movie opens with the Macy's Thanksgiving Day Parade, it seems a great way to kick off the holiday season. Of course, the very next day I'm getting started on Christmas decorating!

Since we typically dine at my mom's house I keep my Thanksgiving decor on the light side. Considering it is a day of thanks, I enjoy collecting vintage Thanksgiving cards and both display them and send them to friends and family.

ABOVE: *This papier-mâché turkey is a festive touch on a side table in my dining room.* OPPOSITE: *This fun little Thanksgiving postcard is about a hundred years old. I love the font, the wording, and the pixie's outfit and holiday offerings.*

THANKSGIVING

A wish sincere I'm wishing
on this Thanksgiving day,
That whether it dawn brightly,
or whether it be gray,
There'll be a jolly feeling,
away down in your heart,
And never for a moment,
after have cause to depart

THU   NOV

24

The greater
the trials, the
more glorious
the triumph.
—Anonymous.

40
No. 20 DANDY CALENDAR
MANUFACTURED BY

LOUIS F. DOW CO.
Goodwill Advertising

SAINT PAUL : MINNESOTA

The same company that made my grandmother's beloved choirboy candles also made creations for holidays beyond Christmas. These Thanksgiving candles are a cute nod to the holiday . . . and easy to put up and take down since at this time of year my Christmas decorating is about to begin. I love how the Native American princess's wick is a feather. And does it strike anyone else as wild that a candle company made candles that nobody ever burned?

Independence Day

The Fourth of July is typically celebrated with picnics and fireworks and red, white, and blue. Since I'm a pretty patriotic guy, I always celebrate. I think it's fun to use vintage paper flags, place cards, and even party hats for a celebration. As a kid I recall the grill being fired up as well as fresh tomato salad (picked from our garden), Mom's deviled eggs, and homemade blueberry pie.

After the meal we'd gather on the lawn and watch the fireworks being set off in a nearby park. The way I celebrate now isn't much different. My little vintage touches are fun for guests and I always give them the favors to take home as a memento.

This array of patriotic ephemera came from a local flea market. The paper flags are relatively easy to find, but the hats are rarer. I particularly love the bridge tallies featuring saucy patriotic ladies; I like using them as place cards.

chapter eleven

✳

FLEA MARKETS & ANTIQUES SHOWS

Flea markets are my main hunting grounds. I like to say that if you want to understand a place and the people who live there, go to the local flea market. In fact, no matter where you go, why not consider adding a flea market to the itinerary on your next vacation? You might find a souvenir or two with meaning and really get to know the place you're visiting based on the objects for sale and the people who are selling them. Flea markets offer up the best bargains, unique discoveries, and often a whole lot of laughs.

One reason I love flea markets so much is that they bring together a community of like-minded people. *Flea people* are usually pretty passionate about finding, preserving and curating stuff, while at the same time doing their share of learning and teaching. If you befriend flea people, not only will they help you find treasures beyond your wildest dreams, they'll also help you get smarter about collecting. Like the old saying goes, they'll help you find all the things you *didn't* know you wanted *yet*!

Find a Piece of History, or Better Yet, Find a Piece of Personal History

I hear it all the time when I'm walking at flea markets . . . "My Mom had these," or "My Aunt Sally used these every Christmas" or even "I always wanted one of these when I was a kid!" Flea markets are like a walk down memory lane, and if you go flea-ing with a friend or loved one, you're bound to learn wonderful unexpected things about each other—things that often connect us.

My greatest flea market find is something I never could have anticipated. One early morning at the Chelsea Flea Market in New York City, I strolled past a vendor's booth and stopped dead in my tracks. What I saw was a large, surrealistic painting reminiscent of Salvador Dalí. I was drawn to it on many levels and while I didn't need a large painting, the emotional connection was strong. I always buy art based on how it feels even more than how it looks. As I studied it more closely, in the corner I saw the signature of my own brother.

Johnny was an artist who, while prolific, died at the age of twenty seven. At the time I was fifteen and didn't own any of his work, other than in sketchbooks I found in the attic. As you might imagine, his death had a profound impact on me, as I looked up to him greatly and he was one of the first people to show me the wonders of vintage finds. This was a magic moment in my life and I consider it a great gift from the universe. Naturally I bought the painting. That

said, I only told the dealer it was done by my brother *after* I negotiated a price! I paired it with a vintage frame I found at a thrift shop and it now hangs proudly in my hallway, where I can admire it and share it every day. You truly never know what you'll find at a flea market!

Buy What You Need but Leave Room for Surprises

Many professionals head to the local design center when shopping for their clients, but I always take my list and head to the flea market. Why? Vintage pieces add a sense of warmth and character to a home. They are also things that not everyone has, so those who decorate with vintage pieces tend to have homes with a bit more character and flair.

I travel with not only lists of items I need, but also dimensions for furniture, picture frames, and more. Unlike shopping a big box store, there are no guarantees you'll find that chair or table, but I always seem to find what I'm searching for sooner or later.

In the meantime, the journey often nets finds I could never have expected (like my brother's painting). Similarly, I've found wonderful pieces of art for my clients. Through the magic of technology, I can text them a photo and see if they like it. If the price is right (which it usually is) I sometimes find a piece that inspires the rest of the decor in the room.

Another great thing about flea markets is that I often find things that inspire me to learn more about the artist or company who made them. When I come home and do research, not only am I getting smarter about decorative arts, but also learning how to spot something that could be rare and wonderful or at the very least uncommon and beautiful.

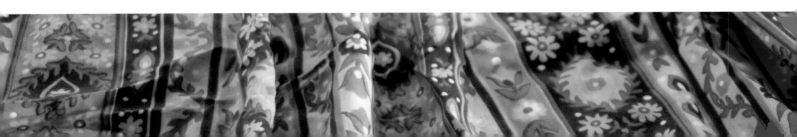

PAGE 194: *Elvis has left the building, and he headed over to the Philly Flea Market. I love how this dealer embellished this fun lamp with a lei and a pair of the King's trademark glasses.*
LEFT: *My friend Randy, aka "Jersey Picker," travels the United States from flea market to flea market buying and selling fantastic vintage finds. The Golden Nugget Flea Market in Lambertville is a hub for him.*
OPPOSITE: *A wonderful Dutch agate laundry set would be fun displayed with miniature ferns in each cup.*

ABOVE: *Flea markets are great places to find vintage home hardware like doorknobs, hooks, and latches, which are all key elements when you're restoring a historic home. Cookbooks are in plentiful supply at flea markets. This trio spoke to me because of my grandmother's Pennsylvania Dutch heritage. Ever try* schnitz und knepp? *It's delicious and you can make a batch from a recipe in one of these books.* OPPOSITE, TOP: *Vintage clothing and lighting are both things I purchase regularly. My friend Kevin at the Philly Flea does a great job of merchandising and display, demonstrating how fun items like these speak to a lifestyle.* OPPOSITE, BOTTOM: *Old store and carnival signs are unexpected, fun pieces that can liven up any room. I especially like to use them in kitchens and bathrooms.*

Essential Tips for Bargaining Success

When shopping flea markets and most antiques shows, expect that most items are not priced. Even if they are, I pretty much guarantee you can get a better price. Dealers expect that they will come down somewhat in price, so they typically ask for a higher amount in order to get what they want for the item. Haggling is a centuries-old dance and an expected part of the process. So don't be intimidated!

Like most things in life, it's not a matter of asking, but rather *how* you ask. Many are afraid to show they like an item, believing that the seller will charge them more because of it. But put that fear aside and show that you like it. Dealers choose things they like so you are complimenting their taste and that is a great way to start negotiations.

Before you start, decide the amount you are willing to spend and stick to it. Also, don't make the offer too low or you may offend the dealer.

Here's how to get the best price:

1. Compliment the item

2. Ask the dealer's price

3. Ponder it, compliment the item again and ask for the best price (might be a little lower)

4. Make an offer a little lower than that (not less than 30 percent)

5. The dealer will agree or make it less than asking but higher than your offer

6. Seal the deal

If the price is too high for you: walk away. If you show you can live without it and then come back, say thirty minutes later, you might get it for the price you want. But buyer beware: the old adage "you snooze, you lose" can come into play here.

One last tip: keep in mind that while the early bird gets the worm (early birds at flea markets sometimes find the best things), late birds get the best bargains. At the end of the day when the dealer is packing up you might get super-low prices. It's less for them to pack and more money in their pockets. This is especially true with larger items like furniture and fragile items like chandeliers. I found one of my favorite pieces this way: a 1930s art deco mantel with lighted glass block panels. The dealer was asking $500 in the morning and by the end of the day, he was willing to accept my offer of $100.

International housewares, vintage bicycles, and lunch boxes are all just some of the fun finds available at flea markets. This vintage Royal typewriter has a cool industrial feel and ones like it are sought after by collectors and decorators. Vintage frames are always on my shopping list. Whether it's a piece of vintage art, a new photograph, or a mirror, a vintage frame is always a good idea, and can usually be had for a fraction of the price of a new frame. OPPOSITE: *Some of the signage at the Golden Nugget flea market is as vintage as the items that are sold there.*

chapter eleven **FLEA MARKETS & ANTIQUES SHOWS**

This is one of my favorite booths at Antiques at Rhinebeck. Vintage tablecloths and linens are wonderful to collect and give as gifts. I love that this dealer went the extra mile to wash and iron them so they are ready to go. For the serious table linen person this booth could even serve as inspiration on how to display a collection.

Antiques Shows

What's the difference between a flea market and an antiques show? In theory antiques shows have "better" merchandise and, as such, they also come with higher price tags. Many a flea market vendor sets up at special antiques shows and fairs that happen annually or biannually and typically they save up special things to bring to these shows. Some are aligned with seasons, holidays, and themes (Americana, art deco, etc.).

Speaking of education, antiques shows can be a great place to get one. High-end shows such as the Winter Antiques Show in New York City are a wonderful opportunity to see museum-quality antiques, learn about them, and train your eye to find them at less expensive venues like flea markets and estate sales (which is typically where the dealers get them in the first place). Not all antiques shows are financially prohibitive for the everyday shopper.

Like flea markets, antiques shows are also about community. I look forward to seeing certain dealers and fellow shoppers who are just always there. Smart vendors also call or e-mail their loyal customers to remind them and in many cases offer reduced admission, while most flea markets are free or charge a nominal admission like a dollar. Shows typically charge a bigger fee (the average is ten dollars, but higher end shows can be significantly more).

One of the reasons I enjoy antique shows aside from the great finds is the entertainment value. My friend and mentor Sunny always used to refer to antiques events as "showbiz" because it really does include all of the elements from staging to lighting to anticipation to audience participation, etc.

I love and appreciate dealers' curatorial eyes and am certainly drawn in by a booth that is well arranged. I used to shop frequently from one dealer who made his booth literally look like a treasure chest that had been unearthed. That said, if it is *too* well arranged, that can be an indication of higher prices.

My friend Victor specializes in vintage signs and these are a few in his booth at Antiques at Rhinebeck, one of my favorite antiques shows. Many vintage paperbacks have great graphics and are as fun to display as they are to read. I grew up with an old blue Ford pickup truck, so this booth drew me right in. OPPOSITE: *The vintage pinups are great for a powder room or man cave. This vintage top hat with patriotic regalia is really a piece of art.*

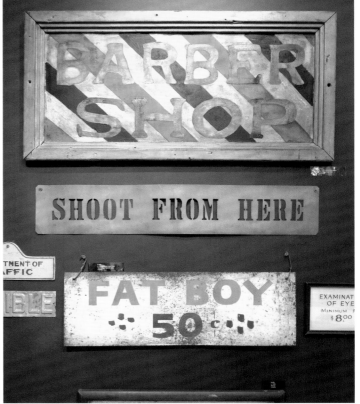

Christmas is always on my mind and I buy Christmas decor all year long at flea markets. The best time to find bargains on holiday items is in the summer months when most people aren't in the holiday mood. I brought the box of orange balls and the poinsettia candy box home from the flea market and placed them on a chair in my bedroom to admire before packing them away. Ceramic trees like this white one are being sought after more and more as many people remember them from childhood.

chapter twelve

YARD SALES, ESTATE SALES & AUCTIONS, ANTIQUES SHOPS, THRIFT STORES, ART GALLERIES & OTHER VINTAGE VENUES

Estate and Yard Sales

One of the best things about estate sales is that they offer a look at the environment where the merchandise has lived. This is not only a little voyeuristic (which is certainly fun), but it also gives lots of opportunities to gain additional information about items being sold. I love this element because, as a sentimentalist, I like to know the history of objects (provenance). This is especially helpful with artwork and unsigned pieces.

Estate and yard sales come in many incarnations. Estate sales usually happen when someone has passed away or has sold a home and is moving or downsizing, but yard sales (also called "garage sales") are just residents selling off unwanted items. Each presents unique benefits, but one common denominator is that the goal is to sell everything, so prices are low, and get even lower as the end of the day approaches.

One of my favorite yard sale finds is a 1950 RCA Orthophonic Stereo. My father was in the hospital (in stable condition) and I was driving to see him. On the way I passed a yard sale with lots of promising looking things on the lawn. Since I knew Dad was OK, I figured it would be OK if I stopped. Well, I found this record player for ten dollars and let me tell you, I play it every day and have never even had to change the needle—and it's been almost twenty years!

Antiques Shops and Thrift Stores

Some of my favorite places in the world are antiques shops. Although they're at a higher end of the price spectrum (because the dealers shop at flea markets, estate and yard sales to find the best items to curate for their stores), the owners are usually armed with great information and resources. At any given time, I have several on the hunt for things for me. I also tap them for answers about the history of pieces, how and where to get things repaired, and what people are collecting. Once regarded as junk shops, thrift stores and charity shops have undergone quite a renaissance over the years. As the name connotes, they are typically less expensive than antiques stores and can have merchandise that is equally as wonderful. As a kid, I would shop with my brother at a local charity store and he furnished his entire apartment with thrift store furniture and finds and it looked amazing.

Auctions

At auctions, there's a fever that happens . . . and I'm very susceptible to it. Once that item comes up to the auction block, if I want it, my heart beats as I raise my number and catch the eye of the auctioneer. My dad always said, "It only takes two people to want something at an auction in order to drive the price," and he was so right. I've found amazing items at auction for very little money because there was no one bidding against me. In other instances, I've lost items I've wanted to someone who was bidding higher, and even paid too much for items I really wanted because I refused to back down against an opposing bidder.

As a kid I went to local country auctions with my dad, where he got me started collecting Christmas ornaments. I still love a good country auction where you never know what you'll find. One of the very best kept secrets of these is that rugs go for dirt cheap. Why? Probably because people think they are dirty! And in some cases they are, but the truth is any used rug must be professionally washed (I travel with trash bags and put rugs in them and drop them off at my local cleaner).

Online Shopping versus Brick-and-Mortar Stores

Online shopping is great and it's especially good if you know what you want. For example, if you have your mother's china, but are missing the sugar bowl chances are you'll find it more quickly and easily online. The Internet is also valuable in terms of getting smart about what you like, regarding both information and financial value. If you like a certain pottery company, you can easily find information that helps you make wise decisions about how to grow your collection. In terms of value, don't look at what items are selling for, but for how much they sold. Most online shopping portals have the function to search "completed listings." Look at these and see what your desired items sold for (make sure they sold and that the listing didn't just end). This helps give an idea of true retail value.

What you can't get online in the same way you can in physical locations is the thrill of the hunt. When I'm in a shop, I am in my element, interacting with both the merchandise and the people. It's part commerce, part socialization, and part education. I will never give up shopping in brick-and-mortar locations because not only do I find things I want, I find things I didn't even know I wanted.

Also sometimes brick and mortar is much cheaper than online shopping and you don't have to pay shipping and you can inspect the item before buying it. Lastly, the haggle factor is always, always better in person. Want the best price? Form a relationship with the seller. This can be done most effectively and authentically in person. (That said, I have met wonderful dealers online and have made offers that have been accepted.) The truth is that no matter where you buy, being a repeat customer is always a path to the best prices!

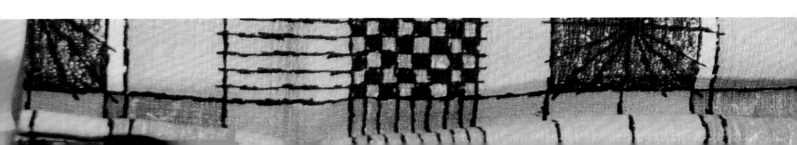

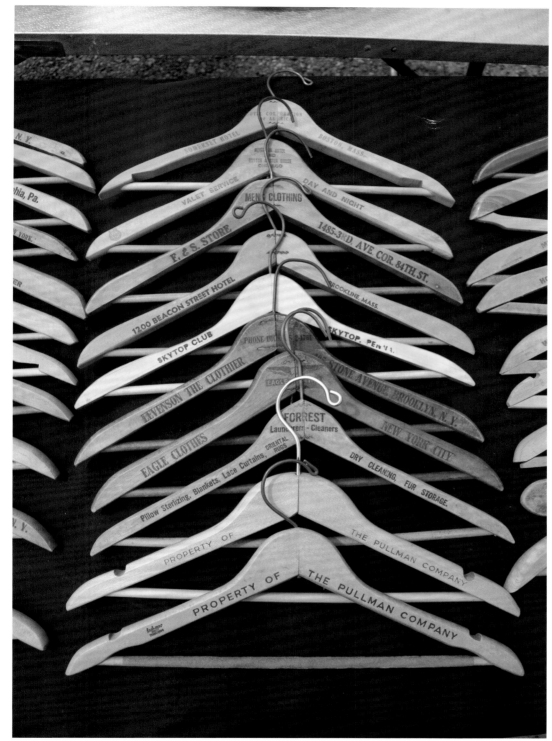

PAGE 208: *A yard sale in progress . . . here the idea is to sell it all in a day or two, so prices tend to be at the lowest end of the vintage spectrum. Artwork, housewares, and antique baubles are all treats to discover.* OPPOSITE: *I understand Joan Crawford's disdain for wire hangers. Wooden hangers are better for your clothing and feel more civilized. I especially like vintage wooden hangers like these that are historically interesting as they hail from yesterday's train cars, hotels, department stores, and more.* BELOW: *Mid-century bark cloth fabric has a lot of personality. Vintage drapery panels like these can be used as is or turned into pillows and a myriad of other creations.*

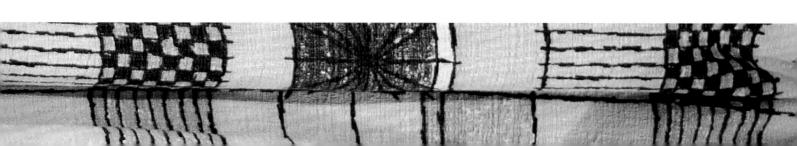

Yard Sales

Some of my very first vintage acquisitions were made at yard sales. My brother Johnny and I would comb them to find pieces of bluebird china for his collection, which all began with a few pieces he found in our attic or basement. The thrill of pulling over, popping out of the car, and hunting for treasure is as alive in me today as it was when I was a kid.

Of course part of the fun is that just as with any vintage excursion you often find things you didn't know you were looking for . . . or perhaps, depending on how you look at it, they find you! One thing I always do is ask the homeowner if they happen to have a particular item that I might be in the market for (usually vintage Christmas decor!). Since they live there, they might just go inside and pull out a box from the basement. I've had great luck asking for what I want and encourage you to do the same.

My town, like many, has an annual community-wide yard sale and it's great fun. The funny thing is that most people who sell also buy from others. So I'm guessing a lot of people just break even, but have a great time doing so.

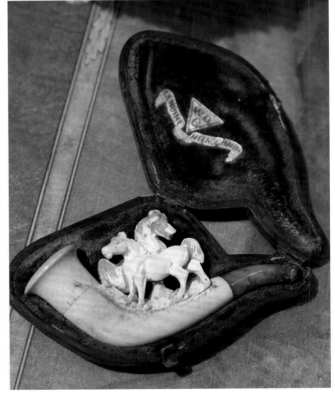

At one time, every home had a sewing machine, so there are plenty of them out there and they are quite inexpensive. I'm happy that home sewing is making a comeback (in my family, it never left!). Because these machines were made so well, many of them still work. Aside from their practical use, they also have a great decorative presence. I gravitate toward art deco pieces and this 1930s penguin ice bucket caught my eye immediately. I already own a version with Bakelite hardware, but I like this one because it has wooden details. Of course, like with all my vintage finds, I plan on using it. Sheet music is plentiful and inexpensive and looks great framed. While I don't recommend smoking this vintage pipe, it does have a great decorative look in its original velvet lined case.

My Top Tips for a Successful Yard Sale

1. ### *Advertise*
    in the paper, on-line, make signs around the neighborhood.

2. ### *Organize and Stage*
    Put out tables and arrange objects by category, books on one table, clothing on another, etc. Price as much as you can. Make signs like "All shirts, $1" or "Records, 3 for $4."

3. ### *Be Kind*
    When people arrive, greet them and also give them space to explore.

4. ### *Be Flexible*
    If someone makes a reasonable offer, make a polite counteroffer or accept theirs. The point is to get rid of stuff and make some cash!

5. ### *Involve the Kids*
    Let them have a lemonade stand or put them in charge of wrapping and bagging. Or do a sale where all the proceeds benefit a family event. My Mom did this once and we paid for a trip to the shore!

6. ### *Give it Away*
    Everybody loves a gift with purchase. Consider a "one free item with purchase" table of things people can take if they buy something else.

7. ### *Donate*
    When the sale is over, fill up the car and donate it all to a local worthwhile charity.

Estate Sales

Sometimes called "house sales," estate sales are fascinating opportunities to walk into a house that's been lived in and loved for years and to buy things from every room, from the attic to the basement. I find estate sales sociologically fascinating, and as someone who honors vintage objects and enjoys learning from them, it's fun to see where they were originally used or displayed.

Typically estate sales are held after someone passes away, but that's not always the case. Oftentimes, people are moving or deciding to downsize. Estate sales are mostly run by outside companies who should have a general idea of the financial value of items, but they are always priced lower than a retail antiques store. This is because estate sales are one of the places dealers shop, but they are open to all.

I've had the honor of working on some of these great sales, and the most notable and interesting was the estate of Rue McClanahan of *The Golden Girls*. While I didn't know Rue in real life, I got to know her by sorting through her things. I was touched by the fact that she kept the prom dress her parents purchased for her, as well as every pair of shoes

from *Maude* and every script from *The Golden Girls*.

Most recently I had the great privilege of helping my friend Tom downsize through throwing an estate sale. A former antiques dealer, Tom has exquisite taste and a talent for displaying his collections. Selling off some of his many pieces helped Tom lighten his load and prepare for a new chapter in a beautiful assisted living facility, where each hacienda looks like a little Hollywood bungalow. Helping him create his new home was a joy.

Above is Tom's new dwelling. While it is significantly smaller, it embodies the look and feel of his previous home, as we kept some his favorite things and jettisoned the rest. The photo to the right shows the painting where it originally hung in Tom's last home. The collection of foo dogs is so fun, and how about the amazing fabric on that chair? FOLLOWING SPREAD: *Tom's former living room in all its glory. This is how he lived with his collections and this is how it looked when people arrived for the estate sale. I'm grateful to have captured this image before the house was dismanteld. The key to living with a lot of stuff is symmetry. The balance in this room is pitch perfect and it was a joy to behold.*

OPPOSITE: *Tom made a grand entrance to his home with these Venetian gondola torches, gilded mirror, and a golden goddess. Once again, symmetry makes it work and feel very welcoming.* ABOVE: *Tom's statues have great personality. The lion and cheetah add a fun touch and the bust of young Caesar sat sublimely on a faux marbled pillar. My favorite piece was a bronze statue of Saint George slaying a dragon. It was the piece that I acquired for myself.*

Antiques Shops, Thrift Stores, & Art Galleries

One of the reasons I live where I do is that we have one of the highest concentrations of antiques shops and art galleries in the country. The selection is wonderfully dizzying and there is truly something for everyone's vintage style preference. Dealers are passionate about what they do and as such do a beautiful job of both preserving and displaying their pieces. Many venues have multiple dealers so they offer various choices and points of view.

Broadway set designers, movie prop companies, retail merchandising teams, interior designers, new homeowners, and collectors of just about everything under the sun flock to our area to shop. Because of the fine caliber of dealers and items, these shops are wonderful places to make connections. If you're looking for something in particular, make sure to ask, because dealers are always out there on the hunt and typically take great joy in finding the right thing for the right person.

Art galleries in my area also tend to showcase vintage items and in some cases the artists even incorporate vintage pieces into their work. Art and antiques comingle in a beautiful way in these places, very much as they likely will in the homes of their future owners.

Lastly, don't discount the potential of a good thrift store. I've been shopping them all my life and some of my favorites are found in our area. Priced lower than antiques stores, they often feature items with great decorative value. Those who merchandise the donations, like my good friend Kim at Good Stuff Thrift in Doylestown, are true artists. And the work they do not only makes shoppers happy, but also serves to benefit the charities that receive the proceeds from sales.

ABOVE: *This mid-century modern montage at Touch of the Past Antiques in Lambertville is warm and inviting. I love how the dealer even added a plant to make it feel like home.* OPPOSITE: *The use of color is everything when it comes to decorating—and the same goes for merchandising. This photo from Good Stuff Thrift Store in Doylestown showcases how one person's discarded items really are someone else's treasure.*

OPPOSITE: *The People's Store in Lambertville is a mammoth antiques and art emporium housed in four floors of a historic 1839 building. It's home to forty five dealers, all of whom are continually adding newly found treasure. This is just a glimpse of my good friend Deborah's outpost, which is jam-packed with lighting, art and wonderful things.* ABOVE: *America Antique and Design Gallery in Lambertville offers an eclectic mix, from large architectural finds to vintage clothing to objets d'art. The 1948 Harley-Davidson motorcycle above was rescued and reimagined into sculpture by owner David Teague. He added old steam gauges and caribou antlers (as handlebars). In the second photo, the work of the late folk artist Antonio Romano is given a place of honor in a vintage frame.* FOLLOWING SPREAD: *Kelly Sullivan Fine Art, located on the top floor of the People's Store, truly embodies the feel of a salon. Kelly's art, much of which is inspired by her world travels, beautifully captures light and subject.*

TOP: *At America Antiques and Design, a nineteenth-century French clock tower dial takes center stage on the second floor. Adding one of these to an interior makes a bold, impactful statement.* BOTTOM: *A large antique carved wooden Buddha and a 1930s "Father Divine" billboard create an intriguing vignette of vintage devotional objects. Back at Good Stuff Thrift, this statue of a young boy is a great decorative find.*

TOP: *America Antiques and Design's owner David Teague made this sensational custom desk from a 1961 Chrysler New Yorker. When you visit the gallery, this is typically where David can be found.* BOTTOM: *Eleanor Voorhees Fine Art Gallery, also located in the People's Store, showcases her mixed media works, many of which incorporate rescued objects and flea market finds. Eleanor creates a warm, welcoming space with a decidedly vintage vibe.*

TOP LEFT: *An old case of Coca-Cola bottles takes on an unexpected new life as accent lighting.* BOTTOM RIGHT: *The retro phones actually work at Vintage Vibe as do the radios.* TOP LEFT: *An old Volkswagen trunk becomes a wall shelf.* BOTTOM LEFT: *An old stoplight becomes accent lighting for Beatles fans.* OPPOSITE: *Another fun creation from Vintage Vibe: a 1959 speedometer is given new life as a desk lamp.*

chapter thirteen

PAYING IT FORWARD

Part of the *Vintage Living* mentality is the understanding that "stuff" outlives us. I love the idea that I'm often rescuing, caring for, and curating things so that future generations will enjoy them. After all, that's what was done for me by the countless people who used to own the treasures I've purchased over the years.

Often I'll own something for a short time but I'll learn a great deal by researching it and learning about how it was made before passing it along to a friend or client. With other things, I will enjoy them for years but then decide it's time to change things up, so I put them back into the world. In this chapter I'll touch upon ways to care for your treasured items and ensure that they have a long, happy life.

Sometimes I'll even give away a piece I still very much enjoy—and I'll take great pleasure in doing so as it allows me to see it take on a new life. I learned this from my grandmother. As a boy, I always admired the colorful lamp in her living room and, much to my delight, when my grandmother came to visit me in my first real New York apartment she brought it along as a gift.

While that lamp (pictured in Chapter One) doesn't hold an enormous amount of monetary value, to me it is priceless.

My grandmother embodied pure generosity and her lamp serves as a daily reminder that there's a lot of joy in giving. She liked giving her things away while she was still alive so she could enjoy them in a new and different way. The lesson for me is to give more, expect less, and to light the way for a new collector.

I've always loved giving vintage gifts and I take great pleasure in finding just the right thing for just the right person. I know when I receive such a present I'm touched by the thought that went into it and that someone thought of me when they saw this special treasure.

I also believe handwritten notes are deeply important in this digital world. While a greeting card or letter might not actually be vintage, the activity of writing is becoming a somewhat lost part of our culture and I like to do my part to ensure it makes a comeback. Like so many things in this book, it falls under the category of embracing "vintage ways." In my opinion, these activities not only help us connect to others, but to ourselves as well.

Dear Mom,
Thanks for
giving me
ROOTS
and
WINGS
Love,
Bobby

PAGE 230: *A bouquet of roses from the grocery store become an even better gift when presented in a vintage vase.* OPPOSITE: *The wonderful people who owned my home for eighty-three years before I arrived owned a legendary Greek restaurant in town. This is one of many photos they generously gave me. While of course I love seeing what my home looked like once upon a time, I also love seeing who lived there. Third and fourth in from the top are Christos and Emma Mike, and the three little girls in the front are their daughters Mary, Dessie, and Betty. The rest are their dear friends who clearly knew how to have fun!* LEFT: *Writing notes to those I love is an important practice for me—and one I learned from my grandmother and mother. I love doing so on proper stationery and am grateful to my dear friend Mollie for gifting this set to me.* BELOW: *The detail below shows a joyful 1970s crocheted daisy shawl, a fun gift for a friend who loves and wears vintage clothing.*

Giving a Vintage Gift

Since I live a vintage lifestyle, I'm always around wonderful objects, many of which speak to me on behalf of friends and loved ones. Vintage jewelry is at every vintage venue, and whether it's a necklace, earrings, or cufflinks, I find people really appreciate these pieces.

In this day and age fewer and fewer people have framed photos. I routinely buy wonderful vintage frames and marry them to photographs I find on friends' social media pages. It's an unexpected and very appreciated gift. The framed photo of my grandparents on New Year's Eve in the 1950s is a gift I gave myself.

Vintage wedding cake toppers are fun gifts to give either as a gag or as actual cake adornments for a bridal shower or a groom's party. This 1970s version is all about his sideburns. What to get the person who has everything? How about a vintage table crumb sweeper? I found this one, a cute 1930s bulldog, in its original box!

Recycling & Caring for Vintage Pieces

I love the beautiful patina of age. I usually don't want to give pieces a new coat of paint or significantly rework them. The wonderful portrait in my dining room was all but destroyed when I found it. Yet something made me want to save him. When I had it cleaned and restored a signature was revealed. As it turns out, this is a self-portrait of John Dabour, who painted two U. S. presidents and whose works hang in museums like the Smithsonian National Portrait Gallery in Washington, DC.

My regular "uniform" consists of these WWII combat boots and this vintage Gucci bag. Both require regular care. My amazing cobbler Arty waxes and resoles the boots regularly. He also cleaned and waxed the bag. Similarly, gently dusting, cleaning, or laundering vintage items makes them fresh and relevant, without compromising their integrity and beauty.

A Panorama of American Film NOIR   Borde & Chaumeton

I Can't Wait Until Tomorrow 'Cause I Get Better-Looking Every Day
by Joe Willie Namath

THE WISDOM OF NOT KNOWING

KILLER STUFF and TONS OF MONEY

SECRETS OF THE DARK CHAMBER

The JEWISH COOK BOOK

The HERMIT of GORDON'S CREEK
by Hugh Lloyd

ALONG THE WAY

WHERE TO SHOP

I visit flea markets wherever I go. I consider no vacation complete without visiting one.
Below is a list of the flea markets in the United States I consider the very best.
I hope you get to visit each and every one!

Alameda, California
http://alamedapointantiquesfaire.com

Los Angeles, California
http://melrosetradingpost.org

Pasadena, California
http://www.rosebowlstadium.com/events/flea-market

Long Beach, California
http://www.longbeachantiquemarket.com

New Milford, Connecticut
http://www.etflea.com

Miami, Florida
http://www.lincolnroadmall.info/
lincoln-road-antique-flea-market-sunday-schedule/

Atlanta, Georgia
http://www.lakewoodantiques.com

Chicago, Illinois
http://www.randolphstreetmarket.com/chicagoantiquemarket/

Burlington, Kentucky
http://www.burlingtonantiqueshow.com

Brimfield, Massachusetts
http://www.brimfieldshow.com

Lambertville, New Jersey
http://gnflea.com

Santa Fe, New Mexico
http://www.santafeflea.com

Brooklyn, New York
http://brooklynflea.com

New York, New York
http://www.annexmarkets.com/chelsea-flea-market/

Springfield, Ohio
http://www.springfieldantiqueshow.com

Kutztown, Pennsylvania
http://www.renningers.net

Philadelphia, Pennsylvania
http://www.philafleamarkets.org

Canton, Texas
http://www.firstmondaycanton.com

Washington, DC
http://www.thebigfleamarket.com/dc-show/

OPPOSITE: *I stopped in my tracks when I spied this portrait at the Golden Nugget Flea Market. Her quiet strength and dignity is palpable. A few tables away at the same market I found the modernist sculpture. The books are an ever-growing, ever-rotating collection.* LEFT: *This little football player taking a nap is so random and cute, I had to find a spot for him in my kitchen.*

Bob Richter is an interior designer, stylist, and vintage lifestyle expert and the author of *A Very Vintage Christmas*. For more than forty years, he has been visiting flea markets and auctions. He hosts the web series "Flea Market Minute," where he travels to vintage venues worldwide, and is a frequent contributor to *HuffPost* where he writes about the arts, vintage wares, and collecting. He starred in the PBS series "Market Warriors" and prior to that was the host of "Minute Makeover" on ShelterPop, where he inexpensively transformed rooms. He is also a tastemaker on the high-end shopping portal One King's Lane.

Richter is regularly featured in media outlets including the *New York Times*, *Entertainment Weekly*, The Associated Press, *House Beautiful*, PARADE magazine, HGTV, ABC, CBS, and The Hallmark Channel, where he delights in sharing antiques, design, and bargaining advice.

Acknowledgments

Vintage Living really is a mirror of my world. As such, it's impossible to thank everyone who helped make this possible—I want to gratefully acknowledge all those out there who've rescued and honored beautiful things from the past and who've kept their history and integrity alive for today's world. You are historians, sociologists, sentimentalists, curators, and kindred spirits.

I want to thank my sister, Robin, who made all of the window treatments in my home, working tirelessly so that my vision would be actualized and recorded on these pages. I also want to thank my mom, who tells everyone she meets that she has to stay alive to see this book published. Now we need to set another benchmark, Mom!

For my friend and mentor, Christopher Radko, thank you for believing in me and encouraging me. For Jay Kumar, thank you for always helping me see the light. For Sharon DellaPiazza; Mollie Middleton, Clint and Amy Henderson; Christina and Chuck McNamee; Karl Horan, Kim Black, and Sefton Vergano: thank you for encouraging me and for always showing up when I need an Earth Angel or two.

My photographers and good friends Daniel Yund and Blake Drummond: you make every moment count. Your talent is great, and your friendship is invaluable to me. Laughing our way through photo shoots made the hours fly by. Your magnificent contribution to this book is on every page.

And for my dream team at Rizzoli: my superb editor, Ellen Nidy, and my dynamite graphic artist, Kayleigh Jankowski, thank you for helping me bring this book to life and for caring so much about the outcome.

For the homeowners and friends featured in this book, Anita and Max Crandall, Pat and Bruce Hamilton, Larry Keller, Linda Kenyon, Lelia and Paul Matthews, and Babs Zimmerman: I love the way you live. Thank you for letting me share it with the world.

For the shopping venues we captured: America Designs, Antiques at Rhinebeck, Eleanor Voorhees Fine Art, The Golden Nugget, Good Stuff Thrift, Kelly Sullivan Fine Art, The People's Store, The Philly Flea, and A Touch of the Past: thank you for opening your doors to us and sharing your great talent and treasures.

And last, but most certainly not least, for those who've crossed over: Nana, Johnny, Walter, Sunny, and Dad . . . you're with me every day, in my life and in my work. I can trace so much of the best of who I am back to you. Your talent lives on.

First published in the United States of America in 2018 by
Rizzoli International Publications, Inc.
300 Park Avenue South, New York, NY 10010
www.rizzoliusa.com

Principal photography by Daniel Yund with assistant photography by Blake Drummond

Book design by Kayleigh Jankowski
Rizzoli editor: Ellen Nidy

2019 2020 2021 2022 2023 / 10 9 8 7 6 5 4 3 2 1

ISBN-13: 978-0-8478-6531-4

Library of Congress Control Number: 2018962171

Printed and bound in China
Distributed to the U.S. trade by Random House